SYNOPSIS

This an allegorical tale about two investors, **Opie the Optimist** and **Peter the Pessimist.** The story mainly focuses on Opie who has had a crisis of confidence as a result of the year 2000 tech stock crash.

We follow Opie as he tries to deal with his — and the market's dilemma. Unexpectedly he meets a mystical, talking Wall Street Bull at the zoo. Opie's shock intensifies as two of the bull's associates arrive to help explain the true nature of investing.

Through Opie's daily experiences and "BULL-et Points" the Wall Street Bull sends to him, we are made aware of meaningful facts about investing — everything from investing in winners to how to cut losses in case of market downturns.

The allegory's point: Optimism by itself will not fill a portfolio, but pessimism is likely to leave it half empty. Market difficulties and human nature make it is easy for investors to lose conviction and thus in turn lose commitment to the investment portfolio. Therefore, filling a portfolio calls for focus, concentration, realistic expectations, discipline and common sense. Keeping your portfolio filled is achieved through the constant attainment of investment knowledge and investment perspective that comes from independence of thought.

At the end of the tale, Opie's Wall Street education is summarized in a chapter called **No Bull** *Investment Points*.

IS YOUR PORTFOLIO HALF-FULL OR HALF-EMPTY?

An Investment Allegory

By Walt Sokira

A SPECIAL LIMITED EDITION

PUBLISHED BY

Palisade Business Press

PBP

Palisade Business Press is a division of Palisade Press, Inc.

Published by PBP. Printed in the United States of America. For information write to Palisade Press, PO Box 8358, Jersey City, New Jersey 07308-8358.

PRINTED IN THE UNITED STATES OF AMERICA
A SPECIAL LIMITED EDITION
ISBN: 1-893958-83-3

This book is dedicated

to the love of my life,

JENNIFER KAY SOKIRA

Those graceful acts,

Those thousand decencies, that daily flow

From all her words and actions, mixed with love

And sweet compliance, which declare unfeigned

Union of mind, or in us both one soul.

John Milton (1608-74) English Poet.

Adam in Paradise Lost, bk. 8, describing Eve.

. . . and to our children

ABBY, KEVIN, PAIGE AND ANDREA

who are extraordinary gifts from God.

ACKNOWLEDGEMENTS

• Jennifer Sokira, my wife, my partner and the architect of my dreams. I am thankful for her constant investment in me. Thank you my love.

• Neil Bansal, my right hand and often my left as well. Benjamin Graham had David Dodd and I am fortunate to have Neil Bansal. Without Neil's passion and dedication this book would still be only an idea. In fact, Neil has helped bring many ideas to life and I am grateful for every day that we work side-by-side. Thank you.

• I thank those that have helped shape my character and my knowledge base. Thanks to my family, I love you all. Thanks to the teachers, coaches and mentors that have taught me lessons

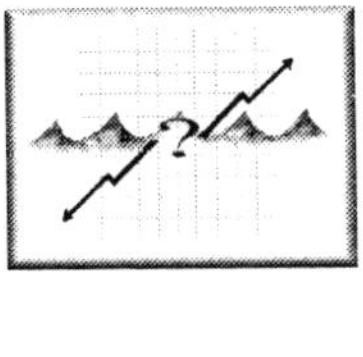

beyond the books, playing fields and routine job responsibilities.

• I am both thankful and grateful to Mike Morgart, whom I consider my brother. Thanks for always being there!

• I am appreciative of all the professional relationships that have been established through WALT ST Investment Management, Ltd., especially to all our clients, and our professional financial advisors who entrust their clients to our practice of private portfolio management. Your trust and confidence is always revered. WALT ST is nothing without you!

• These acknowledgements would not be complete without recognizing some very special people who were integral in making this book come to fruition.

• Thank you, Mark Fadiman for your critiques and editing that have helped produce a book that we are all proud of.

• Thank you Bill Marconi, for sharing your gift of creativity, which is terrific. Thanks for lending your mind and your talent to concepts that shape the pages of this book as well as the cover.

• Thank you Chad Fowers, for being my sounding board. Thanks for listening to my ideas and my rough manuscripts and most importantly thanks for your friendship.

• Thank you Denton Brooks for helping support this creative endeavor.

• And last but certainly not least — thank you God for all the gifts you have bestowed upon me.

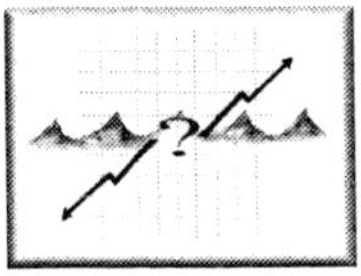

INTRODUCTION

I am an avid reader and a book lover. I can get lost for hours, even days inside of a library or a bookstore. One of my life goals was to write a book, but I faced a serious dilemma a few years back. I realized that the last thing the world really needed was another investment book. The bull market in stocks had stimulated a bull market in books about stocks. With few exceptions, they've been mostly very bullish on the outlook for stock prices, predicting that the Dow would soar to 36,000 by mid-decade and even 100,000 by the end of the decade. My crystal ball was not providing any inspiration. So as an aspiring,

The bull market in stocks had stimulated a bull market in books about stocks. With few exceptions, they've been mostly very bullish on the outlook for stock prices.

frustrated author, I waited for my inspiration and my opportunity.

My inspiration came a few months ago, after the September 11th terrorist attacks in lower Manhattan of New York City. Some ten years ago, I spent a few months working in the World Trade Center during my time with Dean Witter and roomed in the Vista adjacent to the twin-towers. My wife and I love the city especially the financial district. So needless to say we took it extremely hard as we watched the immense buildings fall.

The attack is still unfathomable and the loss immeasurable. The attack struck at the soul of our freedom, but is now being felt at the heart of our capitalism. As our economy struggles, we are currently seeing a major revaluation of assets that has sent shocks and shivers to many investors. Many have lost significant amounts of money, especially in the stock market since early 2000. Those who just a few years ago were riding the bull and feeling financial euphoria are now worrying about their financial futures. Financial advisors are struggling to come up with meaningful strategies to help investors get through this difficult moment. It is important to remember however, that this is a moment, and there have been twenty-three other moments over the past 100 years where events have triggered a change in course — a change from bulls to bears — a change from optimism to pessimism.

Embracing my inspiration, I have decided to tell a story — an investment allegory.

I have told the story of Opie, the Optimist, and his brother, Peter the Pessimist

BULL VS. BEAR

"Markets are never wrong, opinions are."
– Jessie Livermore

countless times. Now I have passionately embellished the once simple joke and turned it into a story that helps me define not only this point in time, but the dilemma of investing in general.

I am an optimist to the core. I always find the good. That optimistic nature has served me well for most of my life and career in financial advice. I consider myself blessed. In my life my wife and children are my first passion and I am thankful for every day and every moment that I share with them.

My other passion is private portfolio management. Private portfolio management is a very meaningful phrase to me, although to many in the financial service industry it is a simple job description. To me, private portfolio management is a commitment to being a good

BULL VS. BEAR

"Remember the First Law of Economics: For every economist, there is an equal and opposite economist--so for every bullish economist, there is a bearish one. The Second Law of Economics: They are both likely to be wrong."
—William A. Sherden in *The Fortune Sellers, The Big Business of Selling and Buying Predictions*

steward of "important money," the money people give their life and energy to attain which represents hard work, fulfillment of dreams and financial security. Therefore the commitment to private portfolio management is serious and needs to be undertaken with prudence using informed judgment, disciplined methodology and thoughtful discretion.

Many people think of portfolio managers as superstars who work at mutual fund companies like Fidelity or Janus. The most popular portfolio manager of our time was Peter Lynch, who ran the Fidelity Magellan Fund until he retired in the mid 1980s. These portfolio managers are what I would call "public" portfolio managers. Most of their job revolves around the priority to generate returns and bask in the celebrity spotlight.

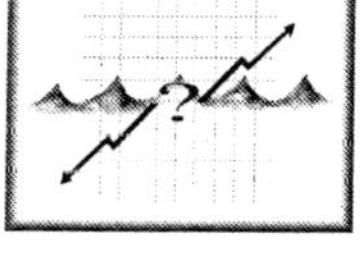

Private portfolio management is quite different. The focus is not on returns; it is on real money growth. Let me demonstrate. I often ask the question what would you rather have 15% or 20%? Most everyone I ask says what I would expect, "20%." I then show an example comparing two portfolios. PORTFOLIO A generated a higher gross return (the 20%) but was very inefficient in growing money net of taxes. In simple terms, the investor in PORTFOLIO A had a nice return but had to pay out a large portion of that return to Uncle Sam. On the other hand, PORTFOLIO B grossed less in percentage (the 15%) but had more real dollars at the end of the time period — due to the tax efficiency of management. Again in simple terms, the investor did not have to pay any large check to Uncle Sam. So the real answer should be I want $2 not $1

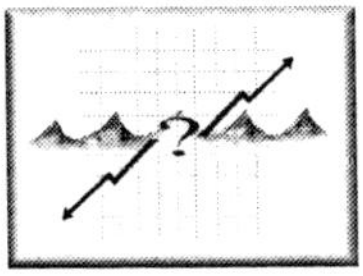

— I want the portfolio that allows me to keep the most money. This is one key to private portfolio management: the ability to focus on dollar growth not portfolio percentage return. Tax efficiency is one of the distinct differences of private portfolio management over public money management. Other differences include: improved cash flow planning, less style drift, a focus on superior growth of capital and a higher level of portfolio understanding.

There is no basking in any spotlight while being committed to the private portfolio management process. In fact there is little time for basking at all — as we are often buried in our offices behind mounds of financial statements, research reports and technical charts checking the smallest details that may help grow the money that has been entrusted to our

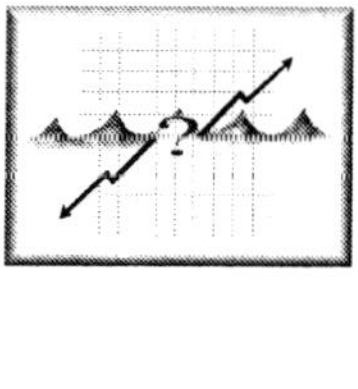

care. We have no time or desire to pat ourselves on the back for a great performance quarter because we are worrying about the next. We realize that the phrase PAST PERFORMANCE IS NO GUARANTEE FOR FUTURE PERFORMANCE is not just a compliance requirement — it is the truth.

Our task is to select and maintain portfolios of individual securities that offer improving economics. We do not worry if a stock drops $1, $5 or $10 because we realize that prices are irrational. We do worry if one of our stocks slows in revenue growth, earnings growth or cash flow growth. We worry if one of our stocks margins begin to get squeezed. We worry if one of our stocks takes on more debt that it has historically serviced. And on the other hand, we do not get excited if one of our

BULL VS. BEAR

"For the long-term investor, there is only one objective – maximize total return after taxes."
—Excerpt from *The Templeton Touch* by William Proctor quoted in *Classics* by Charles Ellis, 1989.

stocks goes up $1, $5 or $10 in the short-run. We do get excited if one of our stocks show improving growth in revenues, earnings and cash flow. We do get excited if one of our stocks demonstrates improvement in the way it handles working capital. We get excited if one of our companies retires debt. We focus on economic realities of each company we invest in — one by one.

This focus on stocks one by one may seem intimate but I assure you that as a private portfolio manager I do not love my stocks. In fact, I really don't like them. This may seem odd for me to say but it is the truth. If I could

This focus on stocks one by one may seem intimate but I assure you that as a private portfolio manager I do not love my stocks. In fact, I really don't like them.

get the same benefits that come from stocks by investing in rocks, then we would invest in rocks. But the last time I checked, rocks do not have a track record or continued prospects of improving real purchasing power over time, and to that matter, only stocks do.

Private portfolio management is dynamic, never ending and exhausting. But it is also very rewarding. We are rewarded by the growing funds that are under our care as we receive a small fee as a percentage of the assets. The more money we are entrusted with and keep (keep being optimal) the greater our rewards over time.

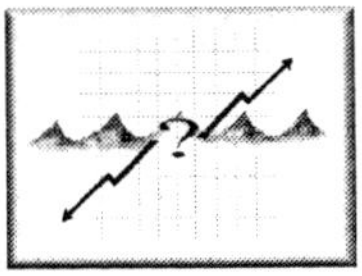

To be a good private portfolio manager, you have to be able to make solid investment decisions and buy and sell the right stocks at various times. However, more than that, you must be able to anticipate, communicate and fight like hell to keep advisors and clients committed to this process. I often tell advisors, clients and even associates that "I may not know what the market is going to do but I am pretty certain what you are going to do."

In today's rapidly changing world, it is easy to come up with a new idea every year, every other month and even every other day. It is easy to be a small cap investor one-time and a large cap investor the next; or growth then value. Investors who tend to lose the most change strategies over and over and over again.

Being a private portfolio manager places me in a unique position where I can view the dynamics of many types of investors and advisors. My experience has afforded me

Private portfolio management is dynamic, never ending and exhausting. But it is also very rewarding.

BULL VS. BEAR

"Risk means that more things can happen than will happen."
—Peter Bernstein
Against the Gods: The Remarkable Story of Risk.

the opportunity to work with many successful people and their families. I have provided guidance and advice over the course of my career to hundreds of individuals who encompass some half-a-billion in private portfolios. People I have looked in the eye and accepted the responsibility of guiding their "important money." This cumulative experience has allowed me to garner much perspective about investing and I believe that there are some imperatives to success.

I believe that it is imperative that you understand if you are an optimist or a pessimist. It is imperative that you gain investment perspective. It is imperative that you continue to enhance your investment knowledge. It is imperative that you understand and control your emotions. It is imperative that you select a strategy that you can remain committed to for the long run. It is imperative that you find someone you can trust to help you make the journey.

We face the simple fact that markets will seesaw back and forth many times between bulls and bears — optimists and pessimists.

I thank you for taking the time to read my investment allegory. I believe that it provides an easy, entertaining read while offering you some valuable perspective and strategy that is timeless regardless of what moment in time we face.

Best Regards & Good Luck In All Your Future Investment Endeavors:

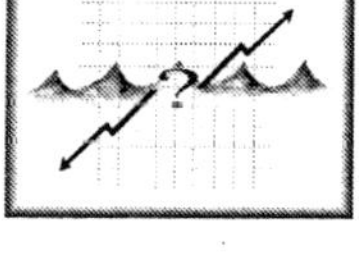

IN THE BEGINNING

There were two young brothers, Opie and Peter, whose personalities were entirely opposite.

Opie was an optimist and Peter a pessimist.

One day, the boy's mother reached her breaking point due to the extreme dispositions of Opie and Peter. She took both children to a child psychologist, and afterward he offered some advice to the mother.

"Prepare one room at your home making it the best a child has ever seen. You must fill it with bright colors, toys, and candy. After you have prepared, put Peter in the room and leave him there for one day.

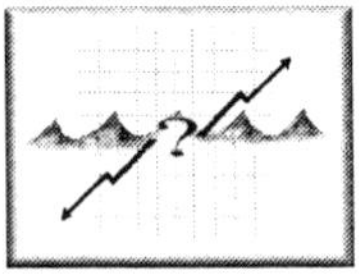

Then you must prepare another and fill it

with manure. Then place Opie in there.

"The bright toys will make Peter cheerful, and the odor and texture of the manure will depress Opie. In this way their natures will be brought into balance."

The mother went home, prepared both rooms and placed the children inside.

Later, when the mother opened Peter's room, she found him sitting among the bright toys grumbling and lamenting as he usually did.

"All these shiny colors hurt my eyes . . . No one loves me . . . I'm all alone, and my new toys are sure to break."

The mother walked down the hallway to Opie's room. To her surprise Opie was sitting in the middle of the manure smiling and laughing

"Mom, I know there is a pony in here somewhere!"

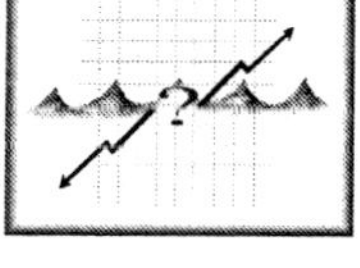

MANY YEARS LATER

Opie walked nervously to the mailbox. Sure enough it was there.

There was no mistaking it, the envelope was big and bulky and he could see the New Millennium Brokerage on the top right hand corner of the envelope.

He walked back to the house and slowly set the mail down in the middle of the kitchen table. The envelope seemed to get bigger and bigger.

Opie had not looked at his brokerage account for over a month. It was not long ago that he would go to the Millennium Brokerage

BULL VS. BEAR

In *The Stock Market Barometer*, William Peter Hamilton wrote, "Prosperity will drive men to excess, and repentance for the consequences of those excesses will produce a corresponding depression… The problems of humanity do not change, because human nature is what it has been as far back as human record tells. Cycles are as old as organized humanity."

web site and visit his balance daily. This was a different time when looking was fun. From the end of the 1994 through the early stages of 2000 it was so much fun. Opie's investment account had soared from $250,000 to almost $1,300,000 over this short period of time, pretty much in line with the NASDAQ Composite Index.

Opie was a New Economy investor. He saw and believed the New Paradigm. It was easy for him with his optimistic nature to buy right to technology. In fact, since Opie used so much technology it just made good sense. One of the first investment books he had ever read by Peter Lynch (Fidelity Magellan's legendary portfolio manager) said plain and clear, "take advantage of what you know."

All was fine and well until the new millennium, the year 2000. Opie watched as the

market started to show signs of weakness. Of course every drop sign was another buying opportunity, it had been that way since the great crash of 1987. The problem for Opie is that he was 100% invested in stocks — though he'd managed to avoid the whole Internet/dotcom craze. Opie had some basic rules. He always felt his portfolio was aggressive but of high quality. He never expected to watch his portfolio drop to $780,000 at the end of 2000 and continue to fall to near $620,000 at the end of December 2001, again roughly in line with the NASDAQ Composite.

Watching the portfolio value drop had

He always felt his portfolio was aggressive but of high quality. He never expected to watch his portfolio drop to $780,000 at the end of 2000 and continue to fall.

been extremely difficult for Opie. As the money dropped, so many plans began to change in Opie's mind. For the first time in his life a negative thought had entered his mind — what if he had really lost the money and there was no hope of recovery?

Opie nervously walked back and forth across the kitchen staring at the envelope. Just then Opal, Opie's wife, came into the kitchen.

"What are you doing?" she asked.

"Oh, our investment statement is here.."

"Aren't you going to open it?"

Opie sighed and nodded. Quickly, he stepped forward, grabbed the statement and opened it.

His face grew long with despair. "We're down another $20,000!"

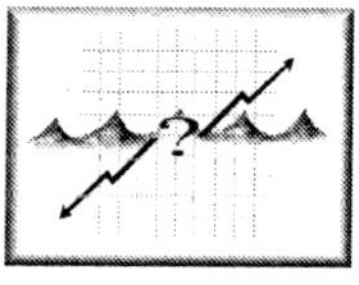

He thought how lucky he and Opal were to be blessed with two beautiful children — Opie Jr. and Opette.

Opal tried not to let her concern show. "It's okay — it will come back. You need to do something positive. Why don't you take the kids to the zoo?"

What a great idea. Anything was better than worrying about the portfolio!

As Opie drove down the highway he already felt better.

He thought how lucky he and Opal were to be blessed with two beautiful children — Opie Jr. and Opette.

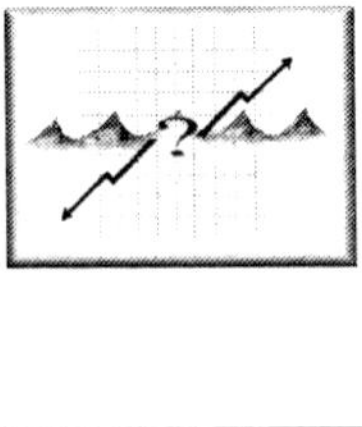

THE ZOO

A Saturday at the zoo was just what Opie needed. The children had a great time. As the day neared its end, Opie and the children ran into their next door neighbors — and their kids — who offered to take the children with them to Pizza World.

"That would be great," said Opie. "Bye kids, have a good time!"

Opie smiled to himself. What a great day it had been! He wondered why he'd ever let that stupid portfolio get him down.

As he was walking toward the exit, he

heard loud noises originating from an exhibit he and the kids had missed.

He walked toward the exhibit where two cruel children threw rocks at a large animal standing in the grass.

"Stop it!" Opie chased the children away and then returned to the exhibit.

The animal turned and ambled toward Opie. He was very close and looked Opie dead in the eye. It wasn't the animal Opie had thought it was!

"Holy cow!" Opie could not help exclaim out loud. "I thought you were a hippo."

"That's okay," said the bull, his thick lips barely moving.

"What!" Opie took a big step backwards.

BULL VS. BEAR

Being a bull instantly makes one part of the "in" crowd. If you go to a cocktail party and say that Intel is one of the best Information Age companies in history and will continue to change the world as we know it, and you claim that its stock price is going to rocket, you will gain many friends and comrades in capital arms.
— *NASDAQ 1929* by Adam Hamilton, CPA, MCSE Dec. 18, 2001

The animal snorted, "Never talked to a bull before?"

"No . . . I . . . never . . . "

"I'm a very special breed of bull. My name is Wall Street Bull. My family has a rich history in lower Manhattan. You probably heard of my father Blue Chip."

"Wall Street Bull? That's — you're just a metaphor."

The bull looked hurt. "Do I look like a metaphor?"

"Why are you talking to me?" Opie said feeling as if he were groping blindly — in a dream.

"You've lost money in the market, yet you haven't abandoned it. Unlike many, you've stayed on board, and you're just trying

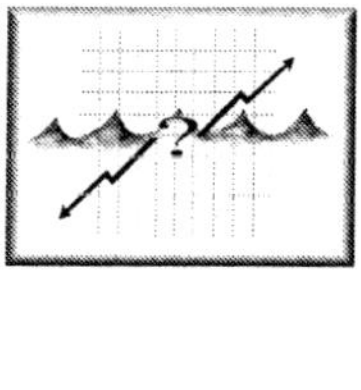

to figure out where to go from here. As the Number One bull on Wall Street, I want to thank you personally for your approach."

"The market has been good to me," Opie admitted. "I want to hang in there, if I can understand how."

"Well, Opie, I may be able to help you with that."

"But why me?" asked Opie. "Assuming this conversation is somehow real, there must be thousands, even millions, in my predicament you could choose to help."

"Well, you have to start somewhere," said the bull. "It's been a rough year. I've got to make market converts one day at a time."

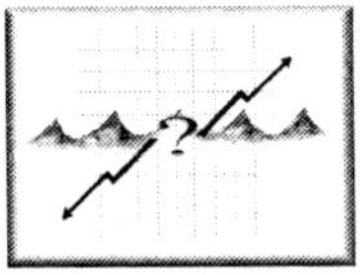

The bull shuffled a little closer and confided, "I've been kind of nervous, run down in the last couple of years. I'm not actually myself. To be honest I lost my confidence near the end of 1998 — it just seemed that the market didn't need me. Then 1999 came along and the Dow was up over 26% — the S&P was up over 19% and the NASDAQ was up over 85%. It confirmed in my mind that I just wasn't needed. I figured the Mouse was going to take over."

"The mouse?"

"That is all I kept hearing — grab your mouse, point and click."

"You mean computer mouse!"

"Oh, really — computer mouse, Mickey Mouse, I have no real use for either. Anyway, I was afraid all of my hard work was going to go for nothing — the speculators

Bull Vs. Bear

"The monstrous 18-year bull apparently ran out of steam in early 2000 with a stupendous top approaching 12000. As we mentioned above, the P/E of the Dow 30 around that top was far, far higher than the end of the 1920s mania, over an incredible 44x earnings. If this extreme valuation after a parabolic ascent was not a classic sell-and-get-the-heck-out-of-dodge signal, than nothing is!"

—*Century of the Dow by Adam Hamilton December 21, 2001*

were in charge. After I'd worked so hard to bring credibility to the equity market! You know, it wasn't until the early twentieth century that stocks as a class started to be viewed by some as a suitable investment. Stocks have always been the jewel of speculators and insiders."

"Speculators?" asked Opie, beginning to relax. As odd as the conversation was, it seemed to be proceeding along normal lines, as if the bull truly was a reasonable conversationalist — for an herbivore anyway.

Besides, the market had been good to Opie until recently, and he still enjoyed talking about investments.

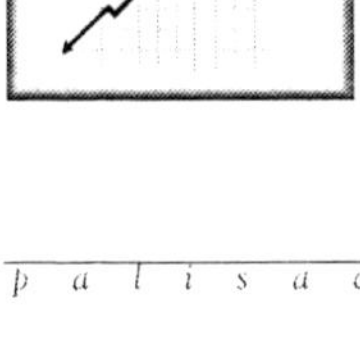

"Speculators are good at moving prices and ensuring liquidity," the bull explained. "They are an odd breed of human. I just never expected them to gain the popularity that they did by the end of the decade. Investors started quitting their jobs and calling themselves Day Traders. Buying stocks one minute and selling them the next — what kind of profession is that? Might as well sign up to clean the Bear cage!"

"But aren't there a lot of successful speculators throughout history," Opie probed, "even operating today?"

"Sure, and there are people who win the lottery every day; there are people in casinos all around the world who win every day; there are people who win at the races every day. If

The bull had raised his voice just a bit, but now he took a deep, moist breath and said, "Gambling is about transactions, movement, hitting it big and moving along."

you want to gamble then go ahead and gamble. Keep in mind the odds are not in your favor. More people, many more lose than win. Gambling is not what this bull is all about, believe me!"

The bull had raised his voice just a bit, but now he took a deep, moist breath and said, "Gambling is about transactions, movement, hitting it big and moving along."

Lifting his big head, he continued, "Capitalism is the lifeline of our economy. Capitalism was not built by 60-second commitments. Look around the globe; capitalism is the dominant impulse of our time. I know that nothing in life calls forth more ingenuity and energy as the opportunity to achieve wealth for oneself and one's family. The momentum of human ingenuity is constantly

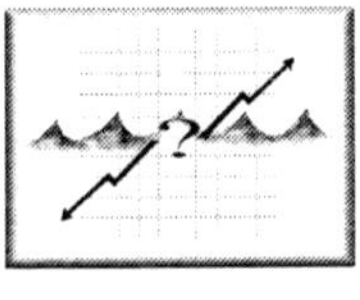

being organized around capitalism — now globally. This is what makes me — the Wall Street Bull — continually bullish. Capitalism is the gatekeeper of our future; our progress and stocks are the gate! My market is for those that want to associate their capital with wealth creating enterprises. It is not made for those that wish to trade paper in pursuit of profit."

The big animal continued earnestly, "Humans lack perspective in regards to investing. Investing for humans tends to be driven by recency and saliency of events. In 1998 and 1999, humans watched stocks go up so quickly it made them forget the long-term probabilities that these stocks are volatile, risky and can go down. Since early 2000 these same stocks have come crashing

BULL VS. BEAR

"Any man who is a bear on the future of this country will go broke."
—J.P. Morgan.

down and humans have now forgotten that some of these stocks represent some of the greatest opportunities of the market. But in the end humans forget."

"It sounds like humans disappoint you."

"Oh, yes, many disappoint but just like stocks there are a few great ones who rise to the top."

The bull turned sideways and Opie noticed names branded right on his rump — the names of famous market participants who had generated long-term investment success.

Being a savvy investor, Opie knew many of them: Buffet, Bernstein, Fisher, Graham, Keynes, Munger, Ruane, Simpson . . .

Bull Vs. Bear

Peter L. Bernstein in *Against The Gods* states that the evidence "reveals repeated patterns of irrationality, inconsistency, and incompetence in the ways human beings arrive at decisions and choices when faced with uncertainty."

The bull turned to face Opie squarely again. “These are great humans that have helped define what my market is all about.”

Suddenly the bull became very anxious and started to hit his massive hoof into the ground, his body started to twitch.

Opie took a few steps backward somewhat upset and uncomfortable with what he was witnessing.

The bull stiffened and seemed to swell until his raw, black hide was all Opie could see. “I must go now!” the bull’s voice boomed. “Before I do, let me tell you Opie that I am grateful for your faith in the market— and you will soon receive a great gift.”

The bull’s voice still thundered in his ears, but all of a sudden, Opie was alone in

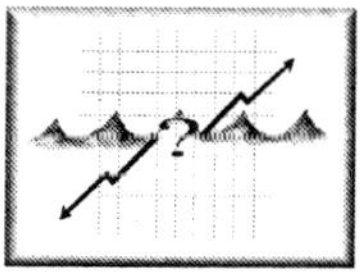

the zoo.

A uniformed attendant was advancing on him with a stern look. Opie could tell it was time to leave.

On his way back to the car, he felt compelled to pull out his new "wireless" Palm PC — one he'd bought so that he could follow the daily ups and downs of his portfolio. Lately, he hadn't been feeling like using it much.

Imagine his surprise as he saw, in bold letters, a message blinking on the screen of the handheld device.

He stopped right in the middle of the parking lot and read it.

• BULLet Point #1 — Wealth is more than money. It is health and

happiness. It is loving, caring and sharing. It is prosperity and abundance. It is knowing what we want and enjoying what we have. Wealth is more than money — but money sure is nice.

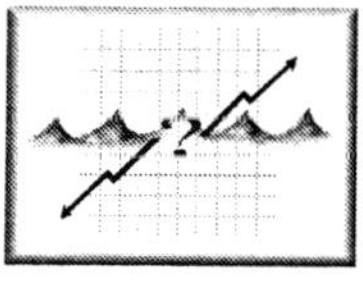

WATCH YOUR STEP

RINGGGG. . . went the alarm clock, which startled Opie. He had not slept well that weekend for he could not stop thinking about his meeting with the Wall Street Bull.

As Opie awoke he grabbed the remote control and flipped on 24-7 Financial News Network. It was perfect timing as they were interviewing Robin Blinde who was the portfolio manager for the Aggressive Growth Gut-in'em Fund. This was one of Opie's holdings.

"Can you explain the lack of performance this year and last year Ms. Blinde?" asked the commentator.

Bull Vs. Bear

William O'neil, author, investment advisor and founder of Investor's Business Daily offers excellent advice for owning mutual funds. He says "the big money is always made sitting tight" and holding your fund "for 10 or 15 years or longer." Owning a mutual fund "is like owning real estate." According to O'neil the secret to success is "you never, ever sell a domestic, diversified growth stock mutual fund. You hold it until you die, so to speak."

"When you try to hit home runs sometimes you are going to strike out," said Blinde.

"That doesn't sound very prudent?"

"Listen don't be naïve. Mutual fund companies are big business. Everyone one of us mutual fund managers has people breathing down our neck each quarter. What was your quarterly performance? How does that stack up? How many stars do you have? I made $329,437 last year; I don't really want to lose my job. Sure I take risks, big risks. I have too. If I put up some big return numbers — the money just flows into the fund and my company and I make more money."

"Listen don't be naïve. Mutual fund companies are big business. Everyone one of us mutual fund managers has people breathing down our neck each quarter.

"You have been criticized for your turnover ratio and what that does to costs of owning the fund. There is a study by Mark Cahart that estimates the cost of trading to be the turnover ratio of the fund multiplied by .90%. Since your fund had nearly 200% turnover, this would be added cost of 1.80% and this doesn't show up anywhere."

"There are many costs that don't show up."

Opie was appalled; he clicked off the television. Thinking about costs made him remember the large check he sent to Uncle Sam because of capital gains tax that he had to pay on the Aggressive Growth Gut-in'em Fund even though the fund had lost money.

Mutual funds have been a big disappointment, Opie thought. He wished he had

BULL VS. BEAR

DALBAR Issues 2001 Update to *Quantitative Analysis of Investor Behavior Report* found that investors average fund retention was 2.6 years in 2000. The average equity-fund investor realized an annualized return of 5.32%, compared to 16.29% for the S&P 500 Index.
— June 4, 2001

not turned on the television as it had proved to be a major distraction.

Thinking back on his interaction with the bull at the zoo, he wondered if his feverish mind had made it up — or if the conversation had all been a dream.

But when he looked at his Palm PC again, he saw the bullet point still flickering on the surface of the screen.

In fact, it would not go away. This rendered the Palm PC unusable, but for some reason Opie was not irritated.

He fully intended to go back to the zoo after work to see if he could find the bull again.

As Opie opened the SUV door to start off for work, two souvenirs from the zoo

BULL VS. BEAR

Persistence studies show that there is no significant available evidence that will help investors locate next year's top performing mutual fund. Bouncing from one hot fund to another hot fund based on price performance does nothing to aid investors in growing money.
— *Persistence in Sources*

quickly greeted him.

These were big, black bull flies. Opie shooed them out of the SUV and drove off to work. Stopping at a red light, he rolled down his window and the two flies buzzed back in.

Each landed on an ear, and before Opie could brush them away, they shouted in unison with the sound of a tiny, high-fidelity speaker: "We come in peace! We can help you!"

Opie's car swerved as he hit the brake and pulled off to the side of the road.

He resisted the urge to swat the flies. "Great!" he muttered. "Talking flies. I must be losing my mind."

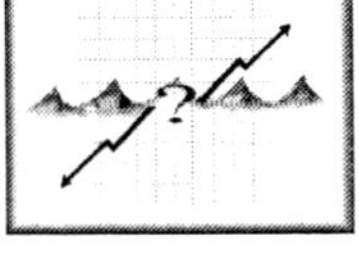

"You are not losing your mind, Opie," the flies continued in high-pitched unison.

"You are receiving a great gift. The Wall Street Bull does not talk to many humans."

"How do you know about the bull?"

"We hang around with him — we're bzzzzzzzzness partners."

Opie thought about that. "Can you help me find him again?"

"Perhaps we can. But until then, we can help you gain some of the perspective you want so badly."

"What are your names?"

The flies spoke one by one for the first time.

"My name is Reese."

"My name is Urch."

Opie smiled. "You know when you say

BULL VS. BEAR

"There's no question that in the past year, the ability to monetize shareholder ignorance has never been exceeded."
—Warren Buffett, Shareholders Meeting, April 2000

"We're here to help you — " the flies said, their voices echoing oddly, " — with your search to find investment knowledge.

your names quickly together, Reese-Urch, it sounds like research."

The flies did not answer, but only resumed their flight patterns around Opie's head picking up speed, buzzing more deeply as they flew faster.

Then suddenly they flew deep inside Opie's ears.

He could feel them tickling his inner-ear canals.

He gave quite a shout. "What are you doing?"

"We're here to help you — " the flies said, their voices echoing oddly, " — with your search to find investment knowledge. Plus we are safer in here, humans have a tendency to want to squish us."

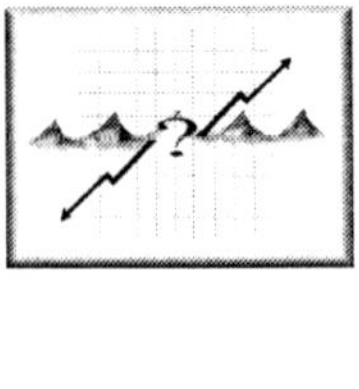

Opie went to work but he was very distracted as can be imagined. His ears tickled continuously.

Opie's job as head of human resources at the big downtown office suited him because he enjoyed interacting with a wide variety of people at his company. He also enjoyed resolving problems between employees.

Today, Opie had a lot to do, but he couldn't get his mind off investing.

Miserably, he dialed up the web to take a look at his portfolio.

The numbers didn't provide any comfort. "Retirement's not all it's cracked up to be anyway," Opie mumbled, trying to look on the bright side. "Sitting around watching the

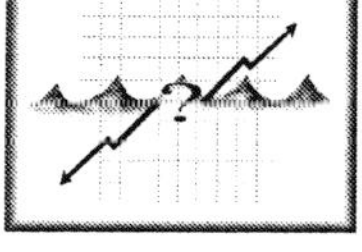

world pass you by. I'd much rather be active and working."

If his portfolio continued to slide, he wouldn't have a choice about it!

The mailroom boy stepped into Opie's office and tossed some mail onto the middle of his desk.

Opie saw a dark black envelope in the pile of letters. He picked it up and inspected it. The only marking on the envelope was Opie's name right in the center.

Opie opened the envelope and took out a letter and a research report. The research report was on one of the stocks he owned, LaLa Networks. The letter was from analyst Fairly Bleeker.

Opie read the letter:

Bull Vs. Bear

David Dreman performed a study of 500,000 analysts earnings estimates and reported in *Contrarian Investment Strategies*, 1998 that "analysts estimates were sharply and consistently off the market even though they were made less than three months before the end of the quarter for which actual earnings were reported. The average error for the sample was a whopping 44% annually."

Dear Opie,

I am very sorry that LaLa Networks has imploded. I realize that you have lost nearly 90% of your initial investment. I am writing to inform you that I have decided due to lack of visibility to drop my rating on the stock from a "Strong-Buy" to a "Hold." This will probably make the stock drop a little further and I am really sorry about that. I realize that you relied on my reports in making your decisions as you thought my Ivy League MBA and my recent ranking as a top-analyst in Investment Star Monthly made me a credible source, however I never really had your

"Retirement's not all it's cracked up to be anyway," Opie mumbled, trying to look on the bright side. "Sitting around watching the world pass you by. I'd much rather be active and working."

BULL VS. BEAR

The *London Times*, March 21, 2001, reported that in a memorandum circulated to JP Morgan analysts last week, the head of equity research, said he must personally sign off all changes in stock recommendations. In addition, the memo further sets out rules, described as "mandatory," requiring analysts to seek out comments from both the companies concerned and the relevant investment banker at JP Morgan, prior to publishing the research.

interest at heart. I was out to make a lot of money for my firm, as we were the principle underwriter of LaLa Networks. In case you don't know what that means — we brought the stock to market by selling the stock to the public and helping the owners raise cash so that they could take the majority of their money out of the company and invest it in better opportunities or just live life large for awhile. We all made a lot of money. You may be a little angry at me for keeping a "strong buy" on the stock as the fundamentals deteriorated but please keep in mind that I needed to keep a "strong buy" rating on the stock to support the share price. Initially this worked out and the stock did skyrocket from $20 to well over $200. Of course as the stock rose it became clear that I needed to use other methods to support it's valuation. I resorted to the hope and pray methodology. I want you to *know that I did try at times to put a more cautious rating on the stock but senior management of my firm did not think that would be such a good idea.*

Anyway, I realize the stock is now at $5 per share and you bought it around $50 so you are down nearly 90% — but let's remember the bright side — you only need a 900% return to get back to break-even and the stock is well off it's 52-week high of $200. Good luck.

Best regards,

Fairly Bleeker, Analyst

Opie's jaw dropped open and just then Reese and Urch popped out of Opie's ears and came to a landing right on Opie's nose.

"Opie are you okay."

BULL VS. BEAR

Until American investors suffer enough to learn the hard lesson that Wall Street exists solely to make Wall Street money by hyping stocks, that it is always bullish regardless of whether it should or shouldn't be based on fundamentals, much more capital will yet be annihilated by Wall Street perma-bullish propaganda.
— *Show Me the Earnings!* Adam Hamilton, January 11, 2002

"I can't believe what I just read! Is that all really true?"

"Unfortunately it is Opie — there are stink piles all over Wall Street. You've got to understand what hands the money is coming from and what hands it is going to. There are a lot of conflicts of interests on Wall Street."

"Will they ever change their ways?"

"Don't count on it. Research is driven by the buy-mantra. There are better economics of recommending a buy. Put aside the investment banking issue and think about it from a broker's perspective. A broker can approach everyone with a buy recommended stock but can only approach those that already own the stock with a sell recommendation. In 2000 there were 28,000 recommendations and 99.1% were buy. Buy, buy, and

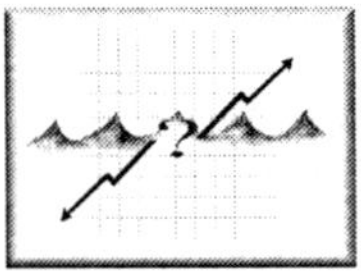

buy in one of the worst markets we have seen since 1973 and 1974. We recently looked at the NASDAQ 100 stock index and found that there are 1,986 recommendation and only 17 of them were sells."

Opie was ready to circular file the letter and the report when he saw in dark, bold letters on the back of the report:

• BULLet Point #2 — Watch your step. To be successful and reach the pasture of financial serenity you must walk through the woods and the fields — and there are a lot of bear and bull stink piles.

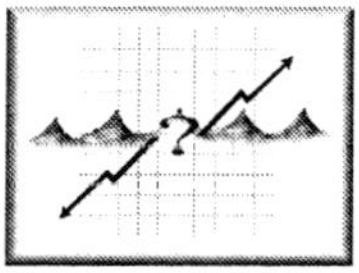

Reese and Urch popped out of Opie's ears and flew around his head. "It's no picnic in there, boyo. You could use a cutip or two, ya know?"

PESSIMIST'S DEN

With his workday coming to an end, Opie climbed into his SUV. He put his hands on the wheel and sighed. His head pounded. "Hey, guys, please — I think my equilibrium is all screwed up."

Reese and Urch popped out of Opie's ears and flew around his head. "It's no picnic in there, boyo. You could use a cutip or two, ya know?"

Opie's route home took him past the zoo, and he stopped by at the pen where he'd met the Wall Street Bull.

No bull.

Opie sighed. Then he had an idea. He'd go visit his brother, Peter, the Pessimist.

As Opie walked up to Peter's house, he passed the PRIVATE PROPERTY NO TRESPASSERS sign, the SAFEHOUSE home security sign, the NO SOLICITORS sign and the STAY OFF THE GRASS sign.

He rang the doorbell and waited. He could see a small eye looking through the peephole on the door and then a voice rang through the speaker next to the door.

"Who goes there?"

"It's me, Opie."

"Opie! Are you sick? Do you need money?"

"No, no — I just want to talk to you."

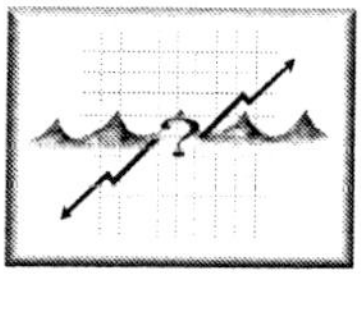

A rumble issued from behind the door,

as multiple locks were set free. Peter opened the door. He was even thinner than Opie remembered, and very worried looking.

Peter had been married, but the marriage had broken up without any children, and he had never married again. Now in his early 50s, he appeared older, slightly stooped as if the weight of the world rested on his shoulders.

He made a good living as an actuary, helping insurance companies figure out mortality rates and the like. It suited his pessimistic personality, since he was always shading his figures toward the worst that could happen — which meant that occasionally his clients did better than they expected. For this reason, Peter was always in demand.

"You know, Opie, I've told you I don't

BULL VS. BEAR

Warren Buffett in 1998 commented on accounting practices by stating, "... a significant and growing number of otherwise high-grade managers — CEOs you would be happy to have as spouses for your children or as trustees under your will — have come to view that it's okay to manipulate earnings to satisfy what they believe are Wall Street's desires."

like unannounced visits."

"I really need to talk to you."

Reluctantly, Peter let Opie inside. They sat in the darkened living room on furniture that still retained the plastic covering.

"What's going on Opie? What do you need to speak to me about?"

"Peter, I need your help. I want you to go to the zoo with me."

Peter made a sound that might have been a laugh — coming from a different person anyway. "I haven't been to the zoo since we were kids."

"Listen, Peter, I mean it. There's something I need you to see."

"Opie, I don't like the zoo. Animals smell."

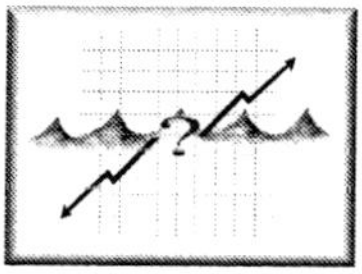

Opie took a deep breath and told Peter about the Wall Street Bull, but he decided not to bring up the subject of Reese and Urch.

"What I'm trying to say," Opie concluded nervously, "is that I've come to believe each of us may only get one chance to talk to the bull — and I've used mine up. I want you to come with me so I can ask some additional questions."

Peter shifted uncomfortably on the slick plastic furniture, as if his pelvis hurt.

He rolled his eyes and blurted, "Opie, I imagine you've lost a lot of money in the

" I've come to believe each of us may only get one chance to talk to the bull — and I've used mine up. I want you to come with me so I can ask some additional questions."

stock market and I think all this stress is upsetting you. If you want me to accompany you anywhere, it will be to a doctor's office to seek professional assistance."

Opie saw that he had failed. He felt embarrassed and tired. "Peter, I've never been more serious in my life."

"Oh, my poor brother!" Peter mourned. "Why didn't you put your money into safe CDs the way I have. Now, you're unhinged and thinking you're talking to animals in a zoo!"

Opie saw it was useless to insist further. "Maybe, you're right, Peter. Maybe I am overwrought."

"There you go," Peter said nervously, getting to his feet but keeping his distance

BULL VS. BEAR

DALBAR Issues *Turmoil 2001 Report* found that In a national survey of 1,450 households with incomes of $50,000 or more the downturn in the equity market during 2000 and early 2001 has been sufficiently extensive to cause consumers to make changes in their investing preferences. Among the changes identified in this updated report are movement away from individual securities and single-sector funds towards products with greater diversification.

— June 4, 2001

"Thanks for the offer, Peter. You're a good brother, considering your basic pessimistic nature."

from Opie. "You need to relax, get your mind off the market. Maybe take a vacation. I can't lend you any money, brother" he added in a rush, "but I should have some travel catalogues around here somewhere. I'll mail them to you."

Despite his disappointment, Opie had to repress a grin. "I don't need a loan, Peter. Don't worry."

"Sure, sure," Peter mumbled, accompanying him to the door and almost pushing him out. "You ever need a little help in the bill department," he said insincerely, "just give me a call."

Opie stuck out his hand. "Thanks for the offer, Peter. You're goodhearted, considering your basic pessimistic nature."

Too late, Opie remembered that Peter never shook hands with anybody, or had anymore contact with the rest of the human race than he could help. Opie withdrew his hand.

It occurred to him — not for the first time — that if Peter had been able to work it out, he would just have shut himself indoor in perpetuity and communicated with the outside world via phone, fax and Internet.

Someday, Opie was certain that Peter would organize his life to do just that.

As Opie drove home, he drove by a large billboard that read:

• BULLet Point #3 — A pessimist has trouble seeing the opportunities of the market — an optimist has trouble seeing the risks.

MARKET SNACKS

Opie pulled into his driveway and slowly scooped Reese and Urch into his sunglass case so that he could take the flies in the house with him without drawing too much attention from Opal and the kids.

That night, Opette asked Opie to read her a story.

Opie grabbed a new book that he had bought for Opette titled, *The Little Microprocessor That Could.*

Opie started to read the book. Shortly into the book Opette started to yawn and get restless.

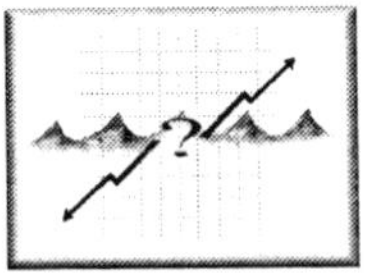

"What's wrong Opette do you want me to stop reading."

"Yes, daddy that book is not very good."

"What do you mean? This is a great story and it has a great message."

"I know, daddy. The message is that if you try and try you can do anything. The microprocessor is just like the engine."

"But Opette — just let me . . ."

"I'm tired and ready for bed," whined Opette.

"Okay, please don't cry." Opie carried Opette to bed and tucked her in for the night.

As Opie was walking back past the living room he saw the book that he had just been reading on the floor.

BULL VS. BEAR

"Never invest in a company if you can't figure out how it makes money."
—Neil Bansal, Portfolio Strategist, WALT ST Investment Management, Ltd.

There were big black letters on the back of the book that read:

• BULLet Point #4 — When the story breaks down move on.

Opie sat down on the sofa and thought back over how many stocks showed real signs of trouble in there fundamental stories and how many of them continued to fall in value. In almost every stock — if he had sold at the first sign of trouble — he would have avoided larger losses.

Opie went to the bedroom to try to get some sleep. He lay down but he was not able to sleep. He walked to the kitchen and turned on the lights and decided to make himself a sandwich. As he finished making his sandwich he picked up his Pocket PC.

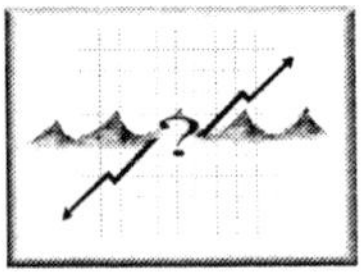

Just then there was loud buzzing coming from his sunglass case. He quickly gripped the case and ripped the Velcro upward releasing the flies. "What's up with that!" cried the flies in unison." You trying to kill us?"

"Sorry about that," Opie said, his words muffled by the sandwich. "It's better that you're out of sight. Peter already thinks I'm crazy — I don't want all my loved ones to start thinking I'm having a breakdown."

"Why would you be having a breakdown?"

"Over the breakdown of my portfolio."

"But how do you know it's down?"

"From the reports I get." Opie walked to a three-ring binder sitting on the small desk in the kitchen. When he opened the binder he

BULL VS. BEAR

"Investors should remember that their scorecard is not computed using Olympic-diving methods: Degree-of-difficulty doesn't count. If you are right about a business whole value is largely dependent on a single key factor that is both easy to understand and enduring, the payoff is the same as if you had correctly analyzed an investment alternative characterized by many constantly shifting and complex variables." — Warren Buffett, 1994, Shareholder Letter

began to show calculations that he had made of the price performance of each of his investments versus different market indexes.

"So this is how you track your investments?" asked Reese. Or maybe it was Urch.

Opie was never quite sure which he was talking to. They tended to alternate. "Yes," Opie said, uncertain as to where the question was going.

"You use price percentage returns, performance calculations?"

"Yes, again."

"Have you ever spent a percentage return Opie?"

"Well of course not — you can't spend percentage returns, only cash."

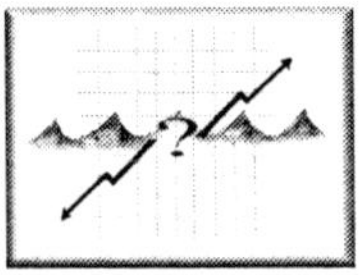

"So why aren't you measuring your success by dollars and cents? Does it make you feel better that ABC Pharmaceutical is down less than the market when you lost nearly $8,000 on that investment."

"Well of course not but that stock is doing better on a price percentage basis than the market right now and that tells me that it may be a pretty good stock over the long-run."

"We are not questioning your reasoning on the stock — we are just wondering why the way you judge success is inconsistent with your reason for investing."

"How would I make it consistent?" asked Opie sincerely.

"Set an objective for your portfolio that is focused on growing money, not percentages. For

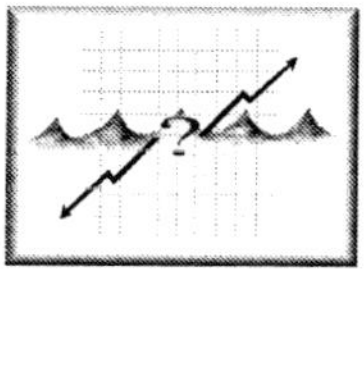

Bull Vs. Bear

"Show me the money!" Rod Tidwell in *Jerry McGuire* (1996), played by Cuba Gooding Jr.

The last 50 years have shown stocks growing money approximately three times greater than inflation, as measured by the CPI at 3.9%. Growing money faster than the cost of living is more logical than measuring short-term price movements versus some index like the S&P 500."

"But everyone uses price percentage changes," Opie pointed out. "I feel like I have been programmed to follow prices. The stock market reports daily price changes and my statement reports monthly price changes."

"Focusing on price changes is foolish. The foolishness lies in the fact that it is short-term thinking. Short-term thinking is flawed and that shows everywhere in business and in life."

"So, if I am not going to use an index like the S&P 500, then how do I measure my progress towards my personal money objective."

"Economics — investment by investment — stock by stock."

"What do you mean?"

"To achieve money growth of 12%, 15% or 20%, each investment in your portfolio has to offer the economic reality of that progress."

"Economic reality?"

"Let's take a well known measure of economic progress: earnings. We know that returns from common stocks closely tracks the earnings yield which is the reciprocal of the price-earnings multiple. So why not benchmark earnings? Isn't that a better measure than price?"

"So what you're saying is that if the stocks I select for my portfolio have earnings yield 12% then I can expect my money to grow at 12% over the long-term."

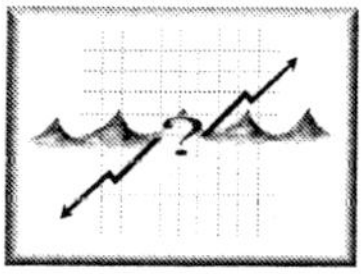

"This reasoning is more rooted in reality — but we would suggest that you do not stop with just earnings. Select stocks that have improving economics in terms of rising sales, improving profit margins, low or no debt, a well-managed capital investment rate, efficiency with working capital and of course growth in cash flows."

"This seems hard to apply."

"It is hard because most people benchmark using price percentage change. Benchmarking using economic progress is different and being different is hard. Go back to the S&P 500, isn't that a measuring stick of 500

"Select stocks that have improving economics in terms of rising sales, improving profit margins, low or no debt, a well-managed capital investment rate, efficiency with working capital and of course growth in cash flows."

companies and each with it's own economic returns."

"Yes."

"Then the only way to outperform the S&P 500 Index over time is to select stocks of companies with better economics than the index."

"So using good selection is the key to growing my money?"

"Selection is one key and art of diversification is the other."

"You mean asset allocation, right?"

"No we mean diversification. We are not big fans of asset allocation the way that it's preached these days. It tries to look a lot like science and investing is art, not science. Truth is, a lot of time is wasted looking at the impact of

BULL VS. BEAR

The classic asset allocation strategy innovated by Harry Markowitz in the 1950s and extended by Roger Ibbotson in the 1990s has underperfomed the S&P 500 by a wide margin in this great bull market. Most investors would immediately disregard the theory as failure and seek out the next new hot investment method. But it is not the theory itself that has failed, it is the way it has been applied. Harry S. Dent, H.S. Dent Foundation report, *The Secret of Asset Allocation*

asset allocation policy. There is no real secret to asset allocation. It is really extremely obvious. Let's look at the returns over the last fifty years:

Stocks	***11.98%***
Bonds	***5.61%***
Cash (Bills)	***5.28%***

"It does not take a Ph.D. to figure out that having more of something that returns 11.98% as opposed to the things that return 5.61% or 5.28% would raise portfolio return. I would say that any third grade human would be able to grasp this concept.

"Sophisticated asset allocation came about after the '73-'74 bear market. The investment community needed a more sophisticated way to pander to the investors fear. Going into '73-'74, most pension funds were 90% stocks. It

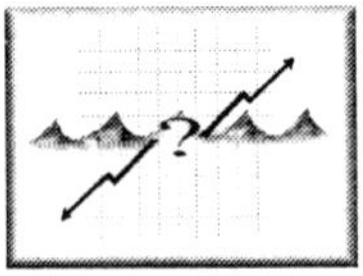

was only after the great fluctuation of that time that asset allocation policy gained popularity. This is when all the hocus-pocus, voodoo stuff started — the idea that somehow you could mix asset classes together and get higher returns and lower risk portfolios."

"So what your saying is that sophisticated asset allocation dignifies fear? It allows us humans to have far less stock exposure than what we need and makes it all okay because asset allocation says it is okay?"

"You got it Opie. Therefore the real question of asset allocation policy is how much you wish to forego in the proven returns of stocks in order to protect from the proven volatility of stocks. The true benefit of asset allocation is reducing some of the overall volatility of a portfolio but this can be achieved through the art of

"It should mean more to you because you now set a goal based on your money. You are rising above mediocrity by not playing the percentage return game.

diversification without paying the high price of loss of potential return by allocating away from stocks."

"How do you apply the art of diversification to a portfolio assuming that you are not going to pander to your fear?"

"You invest in 15 to 25 stocks that represent different sectors such as technology, financial services and health care."

"Is 15 to 25 stocks enough?" Opie inquired.

"Yes, even the high priests of modern finance admit that portfolios constructed with 15 stocks takes away over 80% of the market risk associated with equity investing."

"You mentioned sectors, why are they so important?"

Bull Vs. Bear

Peter Bernstein in *Where, Oh Where Are the .400 Hitters of Yesteryear?* writes to become a .400 hitter, the portfolio manager must be "willing to make the kinds of concentrated bets that are essential if the aim is to provide high excess returns."

— *Financial Analysts Journal*, November/December 1998, p. 6.

"There are recent studies that industry-sector accounts for 50% or more of a company's financial performance."

"My head is starting to hurt," said Opie. "You guys are giving me way to much information way to fast. I'm going back to bed. "

"OK, why don't you put down that sandwich and take a look at your Pocket PC before you do."

Yawning, Opie set his sandwich down as the flies finally landed to their feast. He stood and stretched, then picked up his Pocket PC and read the large black type:

• BULLet Point #5 — Set an objective for your portfolio that is focused on growing money not percentages.

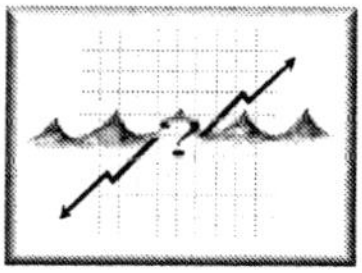

BULL VS. BEAR

"Why not just buy the S&P 500 index fund? The answer is that by applying asset allocation to sectors of the economy that are expected to outperform the market, you can develop a portfolio that is positioned to outperform the S&P 500 with similar risk, which is what asset allocation was designed to create."

— Harry S. Dent, Special Report, *The Secret of Asset Allocation*

• BULLet Point #6 — Don't fear . . . maximize your stock allocation.

• BULLet Point #7 — Select stocks that demonstrate the economic reality of your money objective. The best benchmark for a portfolio is a constantly monitored focused list of stocks with improving economics.

• BULLet point #8 — Use the art of diversification to build concentrated, focused portfolios of 15 to 25 individual stocks.

• BULLet Point #9 — Sectors are sexy and deserve strategic attention when building a focused portfolio.

TROUT POND

Opie woke before the morning sun had given its first ray of light.

He lay in bed thinking about his busy upcoming day. He was taking Opette fishing, then going shopping with his wife and stopping by the bank to see about refinancing their mortgage.

In between, he wondered if he could sneak a trip to the zoo. He hadn't given up on another encounter with the bull. He still had a lot of questions he wanted answered!

He found his way to Opette's room where his daughter sat smiling on the bed in

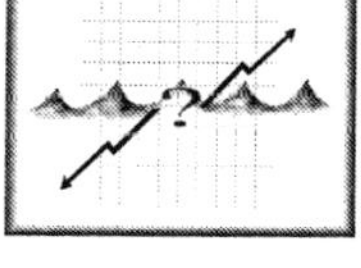

anticipation.

Opie had decided that the only way to complete a successful fishing trip and get all the other events of the day done efficiently was to take Opette to the local trout pond.

Fishing at the trout pond was a completely different experience than real fishing. The trout pond was filled with large, hungry fish. Any true fisherman wouldn't be caught dead at a trout farm — it would be considered fishing with training wheels.

As Opie baited Opette's hook with a large piece of corn, he couldn't help but look

As Opal reached back and tossed here line to the water — WWWWWHAM — a large, beautiful fish hit the hook. Opal smiled and laughed with excitement as she pulled the fish into shore. It was a beauty.

out over the pond. In the early morning the fish were literally jumping out of the water as if yelling — "hey catch me, catch me."

As Opette reached back and tossed her line to the water — WWWWWHAM — a large, beautiful fish hit the hook. Opette smiled and laughed with excitement as she pulled the fish into shore. It was a beauty.

Opie took the fish and put it in the bag that the attendant had given him.

Opette was satisfied but Opie encouraged her to toss the line again and again and again.

With a bag full of beautiful fish Opie went to the check-out booth to pay for the fish Opette had caught.

The attendant handed back a receipt that Opie read:

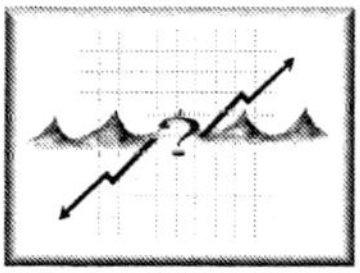

• BULLet Point #10 — Stock your pond. Constantly refining a universe of your best ideas will keep you from wasting valuable time on what to buy.

• BULLet Point #11 — Paying for results is never painful and often it helps keep the pond stocked.

Opie raced home. A friend was going to pick Opette up for a daytrip and a sleep-over; as much as she'd enjoyed the fishing trip she was anxious to get back now.

Opie realized he had to go grocery shopping with Opal next. When — oh, when! — would he find time to visit the zoo again?

BULL VS. BEAR

"Investors have been so oversold on diversification that fear of having too many eggs in one basket has caused them to put far too little into companies they thoroughly know and far too much in others about which they know nothing at all. It never seems to occur to them that buying a company without having sufficient knowledge of it may be even more dangerous than having inadequate diversification."
— *Common Stocks and Uncommon Profits*, Philip Fisher (1958) pp. 108-109.

THE PRICE-WEIGHT RATIO

Opie knew how important shopping was to his beloved wife. He also knew that if he did not come to help she would take an extra hour due to her unusual habit.

Opal liked to compare. Opie would chuckle to himself often thinking that Dr. Middleroad would probably have diagnosed Opal with obsessive comparing disorder. Opal likes to compare products. She would compare ingredients, weight, containers, color and of course price. Opie was her grocery analyst. He would be instructed by Opal to pick up two cans of green beans, corn or peas and compare the

Opie was also in charge of the coupons. This was a very important duty. He needed to be aware of the cost savings that could be applied by using the coupons and factor those savings into his analysis.

weight and the price. Opie would then report back this can has two ounces more and costs 10¢ less. Opal would then instruct him to put it in the cart or back on the shelf.

Opie was also in charge of the coupons. This was a very important duty. He needed to be aware of the cost savings that could be applied by using the coupons and factor those savings into his analysis. The tricky part was having the coupons organized so that as they moved through the store, the coupons corresponded with the product layout. He learned this lesson early and spent the better part of a half-day walking back and forth aisle-to-aisle performing this analysis.

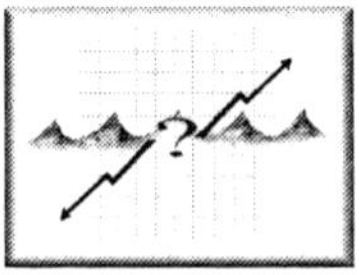

The day was proceeding along nicely

until Opie and Opal came to the meat counter.

"Check the lunch meat, Opie."

As Opie walked to the meat counter, he began to inspect the various meats and cheeses from behind the glass counter.

The butcher shouted at Opie, "Good value on ham today — $5.20 a pound."

"What about the turkey?" inquired Opie.

"Fresh but no sale today. Full price! $6.50 a pound."

"Wow that is a little steep." As the words left Opie's mouth he noticed large black print appearing on the signs in front of the various meats.

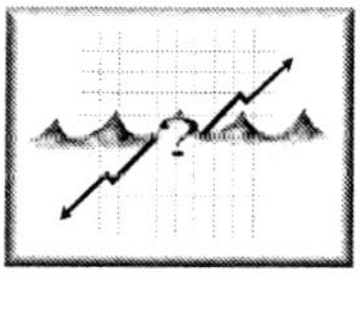

The sign in front of the salami read:

BULL VS. BEAR

Benjamin Graham & David Dodd in *Security Analysis,* 1934 wrote that "people who habitually buy stocks at more than 16 times their average earnings are likely to lose considerable money in the long run." In their revised edition of Security Analysis in 1940 they change to "20 times" showing that you must be flexible.

Revenues = stock's economic weight

The sign in front of the bologna read:

Earnings = stock's economic weight

He quickly glanced at the sliced pepperoni, honey ham and the roast beef and again there was writing in big bold letters:

Book value = stock's economic weight

Dividends = stock's economic weight

Cash flow = stock's economic weight

He turned to see where Opal was and as he turned back there it was as plain as day over the meat counter. The sign read:

• BULLet Point #12 — Comparative analysis can provide

some of the meat that you are looking for when valuing stocks. Take the price divided by the economic weight (revenues, earnings, book value, dividends and cash flow) and compare, compare and compare.

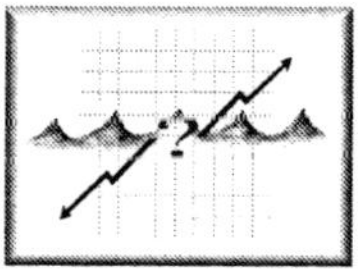

THE BUTCHER, NOW THE BANKER, IS THE VALUATION MAKER

After completing their shopping — and dropping the bags at home — Opie and Opal left for the bank and a quick meeting with the mortgage lender helping them refinance their house. The drop in interest rates created an excellent opportunity for them to lock in a lower, stable rate.

"Opie, Opal come in . . ." said Horace the mortgage lender. "How are you both doing today?"

"Great Horace. You have some papers for us to sign?"

"Yes I do."

Bull Vs. Bear

Benjamin Graham in *Security Analysis* defined intrinsic value as "that value which is justified by the facts- e.g., assets, earnings, dividends, definite prospects. In the usual case the most important single factor determining value is now held to be the indicated average future earning power." He further related this concept could be used in selecting stocks if the appropriate margin of safety was used since it is almost impossible to calculate an exact intrinsic value figure.

"Let's get this done," Opie said with a trace of impatience. "We have a lot to accomplish today."

"Okay first let me give you the note so that you can understand what is happening with this mortgage," Horace said.

As Opie took the note he again saw large bold letters stating:

Pay attention you may learn something about valuation!

Opie was taken back but remained calm and became very attentive and suddenly not in such a hurry.

"You and Opal have applied for a mortgage of $100,000. The mortgage is being written for a 30 year-term at 8% interest. Your payment will be $734 per month," explained Horace.

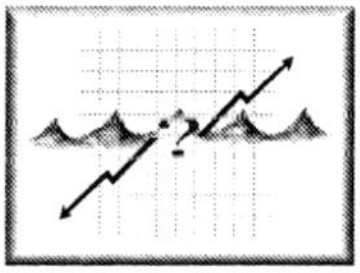

"The $734 is the bank's expected cash flow?" Opie asked although he was not sure where the words came from that he spoke.

"Yes you could say that," said Horace.

"So at $734 a month for 360 months, Opal and I will repay the bank $264,240 over the life of the mortgage?"

"That's right," responded Horace.

"The 8% interest that I am paying represents the general level of interest rates in the economy plus the risk premium that the bank requires to compensate for the possibility that Opal and I may not repay the mortgage?" Again, Opie felt odd because he was uncertain where these questions were coming from but he listened to himself and Horace intently.

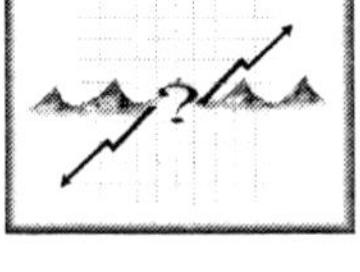

"Yes, that is absolutely right Opie."

"So the present value to the bank of the $734 per month cash flow for 360 payments is equal to $100,000?"

"Right again."

"How does the bank look at the value of my loan if interest rates rise 1% or fall 1%?"

"Opie, I never knew that you had such an interest in mortgages. You are asking some very insightful questions. If interest rates rise the value of your mortgage decreases and if rates decrease the value of your mortgage rises to the bank. Keep in mind the bank will write

"You could apply this type of valuation to stocks. The stock's present value is the expected cash flows discounted at the appropriate rate, and adjusted for the timing of those cash flows."

loans at the new rates which will offset some of these differences."

"I get it," said Opie excitedly. "You could apply this type of valuation to stocks. The stock's present value is the expected cash flows discounted at the appropriate rate, and adjusted for the timing of those cash flows."

Opal and Horace looked at each other with raised eyebrows. Opie quickly signed the papers and jumped up from the desk.

"Where is it? I know it's here?" Opie shouted as he scurried through the bank lobby.

"He's been under a lot of stress," Opal offered.

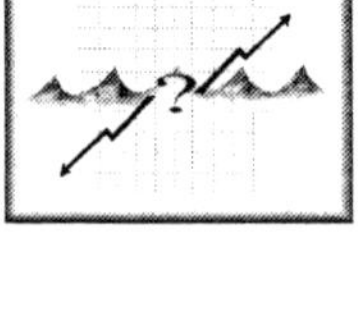

"There it is. I see it as plain as day." Opie stated proudly looking out the large bank window into the parking lot. Of course no one could see it except Opie. It was etched in the light film of dirt on the window:

- **BULLet Point #13 — Understand and utilize the power of discounted cash flow analysis (DCF). For the long-term value of any financial instrument (stock, bond, mortgage) equals the present value of it's expected cash flows, discounted for the risk and timing of those cash flows.**

BULL VS. BEAR

The first investment primer was written by Aesop in 600 B.C. He said, 'A bird in the hand is worth two in the bush.' Aesop forgot to say when you get the two in the bush and what interest rates are; investing is simply figuring out your cash outlay (the bird in the hand) and comparing it to how many birds are in the bush and when you get them."
—Warren Buffett, 2000 Berkshire Hathaway Annual Meeting

OFFENSE OR DEFENSE?

From shopping center to the bank to the local football stadium! Still no time for the zoo.

Opie didn't even know how to bring it up with Opal. *Dear, let's miss the game and go the zoo to talk to a metaphorical bull.* No thanks. He concentrated on the game. "Go Junior!" he shouted. Opal shouted too as her son jogged down the sideline.

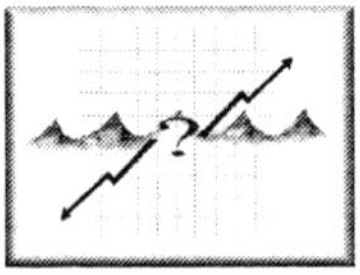

The game was hard fought and close. Opie Jr. made a number of excellent plays, and Opie was full of pride. He squeezed Opal's hand. With about two-minutes to go on the time clock Opie told Opal that he was going to make his way to the locker room and congratulate Junior and the team.

As Opie walked into the empty locker room — the team would arrive shortly — he noticed the team chalkboard standing in the middle of the locker room it was covered with Xs and Os. Then it hit him like a tight spiral on the side of the head there was a message bold and clear:

- **BULLet Point # 14 — Optimizing your portfolio in shorter investment time horizons requires an ability to recognize trends. You have to know if you are on offense or defense with the market, sectors and stocks.**

Suddenly the Xs and Os started to shift into different formations right before Opie's

BULL VS. BEAR

Why should you combine technical with fundamental analysis? Playing the piano with two hands is better than playing with one . . . use point and figure charts to determine when to buy stocks.
—Tom Dorsey, *Trading Tips*, 2001.

eyes — and Reese and Urch buzzed out of his ears. “What is going on?”

“You tell me. Look at the chalkboard.”

Reese and Urch buzzed closer to the chalkboard and watched the Xs and Os move about. “Hey, Opie. This is good stuff.”

“What is it?”

“Point and Figure Charting. This is a really old technique. It has been around since the 19th century. It is kind of a lost art.”

“What does it mean?”

The Xs symbolize demand — bulls buying the stock at new highs. The Os represent the supply — bears selling the stock at lower lows. The key is just recognizing the trend and who is in control. The basic premise of P&F charting is that the law of supply and demand

Bull Vs. Bear

Point and figure charts can help correct the 80%, 20% phenomenon according to Tom Dorsey . . . "the cause of price movement in any given stock is predominantly a function of the market and sector risk. More specifically, 80% of the risk in any given stock is attributable to the market and sector. Yet the typical time allocation for researching a stock is 80% to the actual stock and only 20% to the market and sector.

—*Trading Tips*, 2001

governs the price of a stock or other financial instrument. There are three possible scenarios: First, an up trend, indicated by a rising column of XXXs. From this we ascertain that demand has overcome supply. Second, a downtrend, indicated by falling column of 000s. From this we ascertain supply has overcome demand. Third, an interruption of these vertical columns by short alternating columns of XXXs and 000s. This indicates Supply and Demand contesting for supremacy. This may indicate a potential change of trend, or simply be a continuation pattern (trend and countertrend).

"It looks too simple to be useful."

"Yes it is simple tool but it is also a very useful tool — that is if you are willing to become a true master of the tool."

"What can Point and Figure do for me?"

```
    X
  X XO
  XOXO
  XOXO
  XO O
X X  O
XOX
XOX
XO
X
X
X
```

downtrend

```
          X
      X   X
      X O X
      X O X
O     X O
OX X  X
OXOXOX X
OXOXOXOX
OXOXOXOX
O O O O
```

uptrend

"Point and Figure charts can supply you with entry levels and timing, profit targets and stop-loss levels. What it cannot supply is discipline. You are aware of the theory of 'run your profits and take your losses,' but as you may well be aware, human nature tends to greedily take profits at the first opportunity while hoarding our failures in the hope that they 'might recover one day.' The best part is that Point and Figure can be applied to the market, sectors and stocks. It is really useful when you want to optimize your portfolio holdings using shorter investment horizons."

Then the chalkboard revealed:

"Point and Figure charts can supply you with entry levels and timing, profit targets and stop-loss levels. What it cannot supply is discipline."

• BULLet Point #15 — A picture says a thousand-words, use some type of technical analysis (like P&F) to help you see what many investors miss.

Opie stood looking at the chalkboard and suddenly behind him was a loud bang as the locker room door was shoved open. The team came rushing in chanting and exchanging high fives.

•

Upon arriving at home, Opie noticed the answering machine was blinking. He pushed the play button and heard, "Opie this is Peter!" followed by a long series of hems and haws.

The upshot, surprising as it was, was that Peter was inviting Opie out for a game of golf.

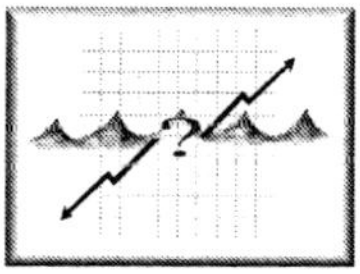

FORE

"Fore" mumbled Peter as he sent the ball rolling down the fairway. Turning toward Opie, he grimaced and spit out three sour words: "$50 a hole."

Opie stood openmouthed, amazed that his miserly brother would quote this large a figure. Suddenly he understood: The wager was the cause of the invite!

Peter must still believe the real reason for his visit the other day was that he was in need of cash even though he had denied it.

Rather than give him a loan outright — something that in Peter's mind would have constituted a precedent for additional loans — he was prepared to lose the money on the golf course.

"Fine, let's go," Opie said, suppressing a grin.

Opie deliberately played badly at first, just to see if he was right about his assumption. Apparently he was. He'd never seen Peter play worse.

No matter how Opie shanked, hooked or otherwise muffed his shots, Peter topped him — negatively speaking.

Finally, after the first nine, Opie was up $450 and trying hard not to giggle. "Peter," he told his brother finally. "You've got it all wrong. I really don't need any money from you. Compared to the losses I've

Opie stood openmouthed, amazed that his miserly brother would quote this large a figure. Suddenly he understood: The wager was the cause of the invite!

taken in the market, this is chump change."

Now it was Peter's turn stand open-mouthed in the fairway. "Well, if you've taken losses — "

"Sure," said Opie, relishing the sentence despite its implications. "But when you start with over $1 million, Peter, you have to lose an awful lot to go broke."

Peter's eyes widened, making his bony face look even narrower. "So you haven't —"

"I'm fine. I told you I'm fine."

"That's an awful lot of money!" Peter muttered. "I didn't know you had that kind of cash."

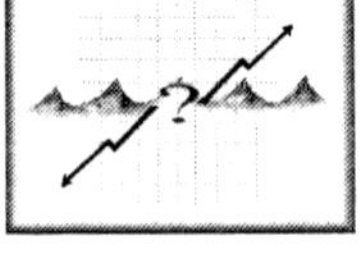

"I don't, or not so much" Opie said. "But I did."

"I don't have anything near that," Peter

said in a puzzled way. "And I never did."

"You've never invested in anything but CDs in your life."

"CDs are safe."

"If you say so. Anyhow, I certainly don't need your $500. It was a nice thought — you've been quite considerate in your own way considering your temperament — but you really jumped to the wrong conclusion. See, I met a bull . . ."

Peter threw up his hands. "Don't tell me about the damn bull again!"

Without a backward look, he strode toward the 10th tee and gave the ball a terrific thwack down the center of the fairway.

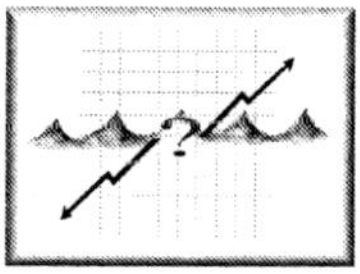

Opie tried to pick up his game as well, but found it hard to do so. During hole #10

BULL VS. BEAR

"The one fundamental factor that drives the boom and bust cycles of our economy over time, in a predicable manner, isn't a matter of politics, interest rates, trade deficits or the strength of the dollar. It's consumption: how the average family spends money in predictable patterns over time."
— Harry S. Dent, H.S. Dent Foundation Special Report, *The Roaring 2000s*

Opie was outplayed to the green and then three-putted.

The next hole Peter won in similar fashion. Peter didn't seem to take much joy in turning his game around. "Want to quit while your ahead?"

"No." Opie said now realizing that he was down $100 in two holes. *If I win the next two then I'm back up*, he thought.

Opie lost the next seven holes.

As Peter and Opie went inside the clubhouse, Opie heard a faint but familiar buzzing.

"What are you doing Opie? Do you like losing money?"

Opie straightened. "No. I thought I could win."

"Who are you trying to kid? You were not very good today. Why didn't you cut your losses early. Peter wanted to stop."

"I don't know, pride, I guess."

"Your pride is awfully expensive," said the flies.

As Opie looked down at his scorecard he was greeted with big, bold letters:

• BULLet Point #16 — You have to know when to cut your losses. A 10% loss requires only an 11.1% gain to break-even. A 20% loss requires a 25% gain to break-even. A 50% loss requires a 100% gain. A 60% loss requires a 150% gain. A 90% loss requires a 900% gain to breakeven.

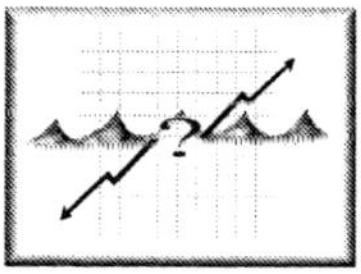

A loud SNNNNNNNNNAP made Opie jump. He spun quickly and saw Peter in a semi-squat stance spinning a towel tight between his two hands, gazing intently into the airspace next to Opie's head.

"I think I got 'em" said Peter proudly.

"What have you done!" Opie shrieked in horror.

Peter straightened and squinted at Opie looking as though he had just swallowed his golf ball. "I think you've lost it, little brother," he said in a fairly disgusted tone, then turned and walked away.

Opie dropped to the ground on all fours and began to crawl the clubhouse carpet looking for the flies. "Reese-Urch" he said gently.

"Reese-Urch. . . "

THE BEAR TRAP

Opie drove home in the dark fighting back his tears. He felt sick down to the pit of his stomach. His hours of searching did no good — Reese & Urch were gone, whacked by a towel. it was eerily quiet in the car.

Suddenly it appeared — the zoo. He hadn't even realized he'd been driving near it.

Opie made a quick turn through two lanes of traffic as his heart started to beat faster. He wondered if this time the bull would appear to him. He needed to tell the bull what had happened to Reese and Urch.

The zoo was closed so Opie decided to

BULL VS. BEAR

Before the problems in the technology sector became apparent to investors, it seemed as though the U.S. economy had figured out a way to grow faster and without inflation. ... A closer look, however, would have revealed that what was prodding the economy ever forward was not a new era of technology and productivity, but easy access to capital.
—*Why the BEAR MARKET May Be Just Beginning*, David Tice, April 2001

sneak inside. He drove to the far side of the parking lot and saw a small section of broken down fence. He was not really sure where he would end up but he just knew it was the right thing to do — so he pushed his way through the high grass and suddenly he was falling . . .

Some six feet later — THUD — he hit the ground hard. Somehow he seemed to have landed in an exhibit. As he rose unsteadily to his feet he saw a large brown bear.

Squinting through the gloom, Opie was somehow not surprised to see that the bear wore what appeared to be a huge but tailored three-piece suit and was talking on a gigantic cell phone that nonetheless barely fit into his paw. He was also watching a large television monitor that was bolted to the outside of his cage. The monitor appeared to be tuned to one of the cable

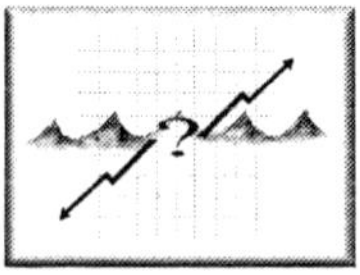

business news shows.

Below the monitor was a brass business sign on which was engraved what seemed to be a company name:

Bear, Mark et al., LLP.

Since the "al" and the "LLP" were rubbed away somewhat, unless you squinted hard, the sign seemed to read:

Bear, Mark et

"Yes, grr-rrr, yes . . ." grimaced the bear. "We'll see a 500 Nasdaq and an 2,000 Dow. Write that down! Grr-rr. *Ciao* baby."

The bear faced the monitor. It was now showing humans in various stages of investment agony.

Click, click, and click . . . one horrified human after another flashed on the screen and

"Yes, grr-rrr, yes . . ." grimaced the bear. "We'll see a 500 Nasdaq and an 2,000 Dow. Write that down! Grr-rr. Ciao baby."

then in a second was gone. Most of the humans were holding brokerage statements."

A young executive appeared. *Think short term*, growled the bear.

A middle-aged couple appeared. *Be greedy*, rumbled the bear.

A day-trader appeared. *Believe in the greater fool*, cackled the bear.

A doctor appeared. *Run with the herd*, roared the bear.

A financial advisor appeared. *Play with other's people money*, snarled the bear.

Suddenly the bear turned and in two quick, huge leaps confronted Opie. He rose up on his back legs and growled fiercely showing gigantic, sharp teeth. WHO ARE YOU?

The bear's jaws didn't seem to move but

BULL VS. BEAR

"Bears scour history and the information superhighways for important information that they can use to attempt to learn how markets work. Rather than accepting on pure faith alone the assertion that markets will rise in a straight-line forever, the bears seek to understand the market cycles of history and learn what really drives equity prices."
— NASDAQ 1929 by Adam Hamilton, CPA, MCSE Dec. 18, 2001

the word echoed in Opie's head. Opie's mouth quivered with fear; his eyes teared, and he felt his leg muscles tensing involuntarily, set for flight, as panic overcame him.

Just then something flew into his ears. He heard a familiar buzzing.

"Nooooooo, Opie!" cried Reese and Urch together inside his ears. "You must face the bear. Don't be afraid. Tell him what you believe and tell him why you believe it. You can beat him."

Surprised as he was, Opie was glad to have Reese & Urch back in his ears. He found inspiration in their words. So he closed his eyes and reached deep inside to his true convictions.

The bear ground his great jaws. More words echoed in Opie's skull. "You will lose it all!"

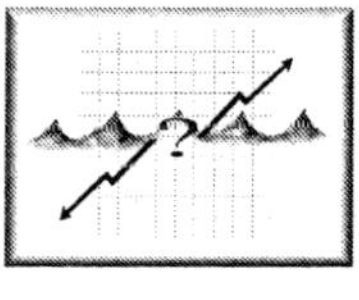

Opie swallowed, his mouth dry. Somehow he found the courage to speak — in a squeaky tone. "No. I won't. I've learned a lot in a short period of time and I am not afraid of you anymore."

"You must be afraid."

"No you are not the reason that I have lost money! It would be easy to blame it on you but it is my fault."

"You must sell everything . . ."

"No. I don't choose to!"

"You must!"

"You know what I must do!" Opie shouted back, the squeaking tone gone. "I must control my lack of financial discipline. I must diminish my unrealistic expectations and expand my investment common sense!"

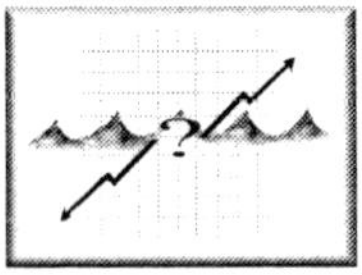

Grrrr-rrr! . . .

The bear swatted at him with one great paw. As Opie ducked, the other gigantic paw propelled itself upward into his jaw — Opie saw stars briefly, and then, just as he passed out, a bullet point emblazoned in the darkness of his bruised brain.

BULLet Point #17 — Investment success lies in simplicity as basic as independence of thought, financial discipline, realistic expectations and common sense.

BULL VS. BEAR

"Investing is not complicated. You need to know accounting, the language of business. You should read The Intelligent Investor. You need the right mindset, the right temperament. You should be interested in the process and be in your circle of competence... Avoid over stimulation. Read Ben Graham and Phil Fisher, read annual reports and trade reports, but don't do equations with Greek letters in them."

—1993 Shareholder Letter

THE BULL RUN

When Opie regained consciousness, he found himself prone on a grassy bank at the edge of the zoo. The bear cage was gone and Reese and Urch buzzed overhead.

His head throbbed. He groaned and sat up. "I thought I lost you guys for good."

Buzzing and swooping, Reese and Urch told Opie how they had been dazed by the thwack of Peter's towel and then had followed far behind Opie's speeding car to the zoo. They'd arrived just in time to see Opie facing down the bear.

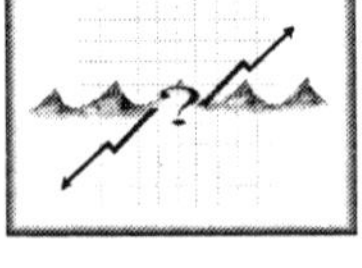

"You did it!" they congratulated him. "You stood your ground against Bear Market!"

Opie supposed they'd read the bear's sign wrong. He started to correct them, but as he sat up, his head throbbed, and he gave out a groan.

"Now you must come see the bull!"

Opie limped along behind Reese and Urch, allowing himself to be led more by their buzzing than by his eyes on this moonless night.

Eventually, the bull's cage loomed like the prow of a vast, wrecked ship.

The bull loomed almost as large in the middle of the exhibit.

The sight of the bull invigorated Opie and made his headache all but disappear. He walked quickly through the open cage door and came as close as he dared. "It's so good to see you! I've learned so much since the last time we talked."

BULL VS. BEAR

"The shakeout in technology stocks has been even more severe that in home-building in the early 1990s. But it is closely in line with the automobile correction in the early 1920s when the auto index was down 70%. ... An industry shakeout creates short-term chaos, but it forces reallocation of productive assets and reduction of unproductive debt that ultimately benefits consumers."
— Harry S. Dent, H.S. Dent Report, *The Buy Opportunity of a Lifetime*

"Fear is the hard emotion to keep in check. Fear makes human do some desperate things. The first key to controlling you fear is understanding the bear."

"Yes. I see you have spent some time with my trusted friends. They are simply buzzing with knowledge, are they not?" chuckled the bull.

"I also ran into the bear," offered Opie. "I still have a headache from that one."

The bull took a deep, snuffling breath of air — then allowed, "He has control right now, but not for long."

"He seemed harmless from a distance and then as he approached he was the scariest creature I have ever seen. Fear overtook me."

"Fear is a hard emotion to keep in check. Fear makes humans do some desperate things. The first key to controlling you fear is understanding the bear."

"Understand the bear?"

"Since the 1950s the bear has taken control nine times — ten now — about every five-years on average. On average his bearish activities last a little over 12 months and take about 29¢ of every dollar invested out of human's hides."

"Since I got into investing it seems you've been in control, not the bear."

"Right, Opie. With the exception of a short time in 1987 and 1990 I was in total control of the market but my run brings the other dangerous emotion to great excess."

"The other great emotion?"

"Greed — greed is the major emotion during my run. When the market is rising, so do expectations. The long-term historical return for stock is somewhere near 9%, but when I am running strong humans quickly think 30% and 40%

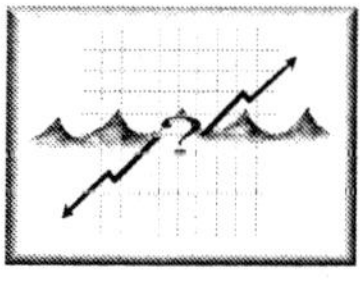

returns are possible, even inevitable."

"It seems fear is stronger than greed?"

The bull nodded and snuffled. In the dirt floor of the cage he traced illuminated letters with one gigantic hoof. Opie leaned over to see.

BULLet Point #18 — the average human values a dollar lost twice as much as a dollar gained. When humans begin to lose money, all kind of fantasies are mobilized, like, 'I never should have bought stock; people like me don't belong in the stock market; I knew this would happen; I am being punished.' "

"I had those feelings when the bear was cornering me," Opie admitted. "I almost said that I should have never bought stocks and that Peter was right about keeping money in the bank

<u>BULL VS. BEAR</u>

"Speculation is an effort, probably unsuccessful, to turn a little money into a lot. Investment is an effort, which should be successful, to prevent a lot of money from becoming a little."

— Fred Schwed Jr., *Where Are The Customer's Yachts?*

— safe and secure."

"I'm glad you didn't say that out loud to the bear. Admitting defeat to the bear is a guaranteed loss. When you admit defeat and take money out of the market you have locked in your losses — there is no future bull run."

"When will you run again?"

"My run, just like the bear's attack, is not something that can be pinpointed or timed with precision. The change in control can be recognized by being tuned in to what is happening and by paying attention to what the market, sectors and individual securities are telling you.

The bull traced more glowing words into the dirt, erasing the previous ones.

BULLet Point #19 — Strategy that dynamically shifts based on what the market,

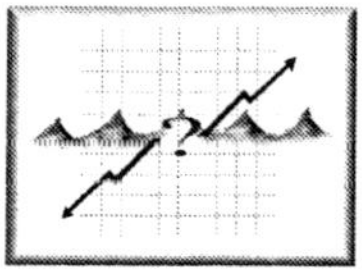

sectors and stocks are telling you to do is the axiom of success. Shifting does not equal market timing — you must always be invested."

Reese and Urch slowly buzzed up to Opie and the bull.

"It is time for us to go, Bull"

The bull stiffened and swelled until his raw, black hide was all Opie could see.

Opie's head pained him with a harsh stab, and he felt faint. Suddenly, he was more alone in the zoo. The bull was gone and so was his large cage.

From far away there came a faint buzzing.

BULL VS. BEAR

"Investors must clearly avoid subscribing to consensus viewpoints and majority opinions for stock market profits. Investment returns depend on one's ability to make independent decisions while escaping the influence of ill-timed investment advice, public opinions, and generally accepted theories."
— Carroll D. Aby, Ph.D., *Point & Figure Charting*, 1996.

FINANCIAL STRATEGIES

Opie walked toward the buzzing, expecting to find Reese and Urch.

Instead, he came to an oddly shaped door that seemed to hover in the gloom above the zoo walkway. Opie pushed through the door and found himself in a formless office that gave an impression of businesslike comfort, containing several inviting chairs and a huge unoccupied desk.

On the desk was a speaker phone, a state-of-the-art computing system and a brass nameplate screwed slantwise into a marble holder near the front the dark, polished edge. The placard read:

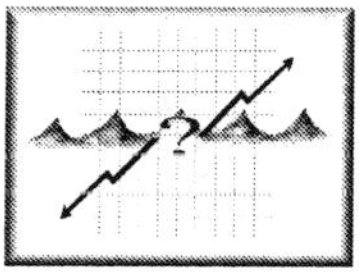

Mr. Reese Urch, Financial Advisor

Opie would have grinned if his head hadn't hurt so much. Instead he sat down in a comfortable chair and waited. He didn't have to wait long. The speaker phone cracked to life with a familiar buzzing. "Reese — Urch, is that you? What are you doing here?"

"We've gone into business," they buzzed in unison. "Together, for public consumption, we present the public face of one advisor — Reese Urch, certified financial advisor.

"But nobody is going to hire two flies as one financial planner."

"On the contrary," the flies buzzed confidently. "We expect to be in demand. First of all, we're not going to conduct any business in person. You don't need to anymore. Our

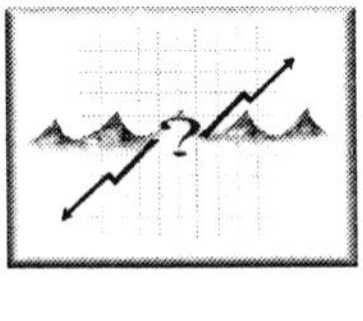

clients will make contact with us over the phone and by the Internet. As you can see, we've set up a thoroughly modern office."

"It is nice," Opie admitted. "But bare."

"Second of all," the two buzzed, "we expect to have at least one client right away who will give us great recommendations throughout the community."

"And who might that be?"

"Why you, of course!"

"I don't know that I need a financial advisor."

"That's the final step in your financial education — knowing what you can do and what you needn't do, and what you know and don't know."

The speaker phone buzzed emphatical-

BULL VS. BEAR

"Games of chance must be distinguished from games in which skill makes a difference. The principles that work in roulette, dice, and slot machines are identical, but they explain only part of what is involved in poker, betting on the horses, and backgammon. ... There are cardplayers and racetrack bettors who are genuine professionals, but no one makes a successful profession out of Craps."
—Peter Bernstein, *Against the Gods*

ly as the flies continued: "The truth is that the financial advisor is like all other professions. There are great advisors, good advisors, not-so-good advisors and downright scoundrels. There are competent professionals that represent your best interests, and there are salespeople who sell the most products at the highest commission to them. There are advisors who specialize and there are advisors who try to be everything to everybody. We expect to be among the best financial advisors available. When we get busy, after all, we really get buzzzzzy!"

Opie became aware of a single sheet of paper sitting on the desk, glowing against the dark wood. He picked it up and read:

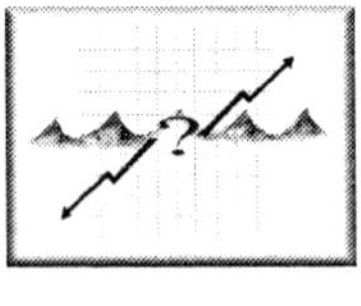

• BULLet Point #20 — Respect the difficulty of working with mass

amounts of information. Few investors can use information wisely. There is a big difference between in-depth information and in-depth investment profits.

Opie put the paper back down on the desk and it vanished. Reese (or Urch) buzzed excitedly from the speaker phone: "Admit it, Opie. You don't know the first thing about intrinsic value and cash flows. Looking at a financial statement or a stock chart is like going to the emergency room and looking at x-rays for you."

"That's true enough," Opie said.

"You don't know the first thing about intrinsic value and cash flows. Looking at a financial statement or a stock chart is like going to the emergency room and looking at x-rays for you."

BULL VS. BEAR

"Trust everybody, but cut the cards."
—Finley Peter Dunne (1867-1936), U.S. journalist, humorist, Mr. *Dooley's Philosophy*, *"Casual Observations"* (1900)

"You're a busy man yourself! Your most precious asset is time. Why do you want to try and manage a portfolio when there are others who have studied hard to master the complexities of modern investing — and who are willing to do it for you."

"I never thought of letting someone else do it," Opie admitted. "I was doing so well in the 1990s. It seemed easy."

"It's never easy for long!"

"So I've discovered."

"We use a team approach," the two chorused. "Sure, Total-Wealth-Planning is a bzzzzz-uzz word, Opie, but it works! When you team-up with two top flies like us who serve as your financial advisors — making specific decisions regarding your taxable, tax deferred and tax free "money baskets" — well, you're on your way."

And the flies added, "As your Total Wealth Planners, we will help figure out if we are using all the 'baskets' properly and if your wills, tax plan and estate plan needs a review."

"And what about the private portfolio management part?"

"A private portfolio manager is our teamzzzzz's specialized money manager."

"Not one of you?"

"Not necessarily. He or she is often someone we work with who designs and manages portfolios for our clients or works with the design we've developed. Typically a private portfolio manager uses discretion in

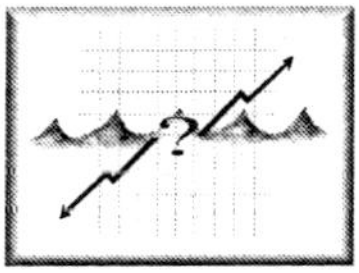

Bull Vs. Bear

An objective advisor will teach you the proven principles of investing and keep you on the system." —Harry S. Dent, H.S. Special Report, *The Roaring 2000s*

making decisions, and charges fees equivalent to a small percentage of the value of the assets under management."

Opie thought about this. "OK, guys, here's what I want — a portfolio manager who understands me, thinks independently, understands how to grow money, has a strong bias towards stocks, utilizes a focused portfolio of individual investments, listens to the market, sectors and stocks, has a strong-sell side discipline, and is committed to communication."

"That's quite a mouthful, Opie!"

"I'm not finished. I want to double our investments in six-years. I want proof that each investment has improving economics to accomplish that goal. I realize that sometimes stock prices will act irrational, but growth in revenues, earnings and cash flow are the keys to benchmarking our success."

"Thanks for your confidence, Opie."

"You better work hard, boys. I've been sitting around worrying without taking any action. I need to get back on track."

"You need positioning for the long haul."

"Exactly," Opie said. "I've been worrying about things I can't control. Now it's time to take charge.

"That's the spirit, Opie."

"Yes, well, thanks to you guys and what I've been through recently, I guess you can say I've recovered my positive frame of mind. I don't care what happens to the market in the short term. In the long term, I guess you could say ***I am optimistically BULLish."***

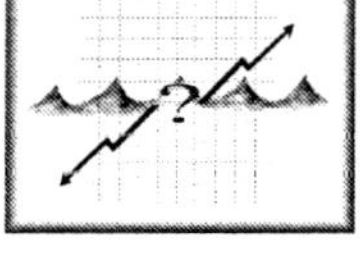

SOURCES

Education is a lifelong process. Here are some of the sources that I have drawn upon to construct this allegory and recommend highly for any investor wishing to gain valuable investment perspective and knowledge.

ASSET ALLOCATION & DIVERSIFICATION

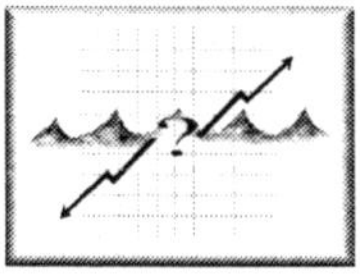

Harry Markowitz pioneered asset allocation theory in the 1950's. It wasn't until the 1970's that there were computers capable of testing the theory. Since then, the application of asset allocation has created a wide variety of processes, product and advice. The theory of asset allocation has stood the test of time, however the application is still very questionable and often hotly debated. For more insight on asset allocation see:

Markowitz, H. (Harry), "Portfolio Selection; Efficient Diversification of Investments," New Haven & London, Yale University Press [c1959]

Harry S. Dent, "The Secret of Asset Allocation Special Report" available through the H.S. Dent Foundation @ http://www.hsdent.com

William Janhnke, "The Asset Allocation Hoax," Journal of Financial Planning, February 1997. There are a series of other articles at the financial-design web site under FD Papers that provide further argument and insight into the issue of asset allocation; @

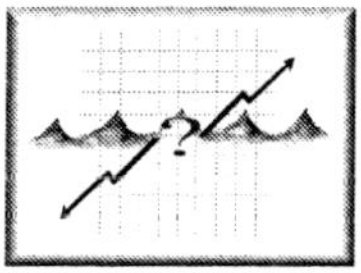

http://www.financial-design.com.

Roger G. Ibbotson and Paul D. Kaplan, "Does Asset Allocation Policy Explain 40, 90, or 100 Percent of Performance?", Financial Analysts Journal, vol. 56, no. 1 (January/February 2000): 26-33

Best Bear Reading

David W. Tice & Associates, Inc., @ www.PrudentBear.com offers what they call "The One-Stop Shop for the Bear Case" While at the site visit The Credit Bubble Bulletin by Doug Noland.

Zeal Intelligence monthly intelligence briefing, the famous Zeal Research weekly Internet essays by Adam Hamilton can be found @ http://www.zeallc.com/about.htm

Marc Faber's The Gloom Boom & Doom Report aims, based on economic, social and historical trends, to warn investors when investment themes have become widely accepted and are, therefore, highly priced and risky, while it continuously searches for opportunities in unloved and depressed markets. For more information visit www.gloomboomdoom.com.

Best Bull Reading

Dent, Harry S., The Great Boom Ahead: Your Comprehensive Guide to Personal and Business Profit in the New Era of Prosperity, New York: Hyperion, c1993.

Dent, Harry S., The Roaring 2000s: Building the Wealth and Lifestyle You Desire in the Greatest Boom In History / Harry S. Dent,

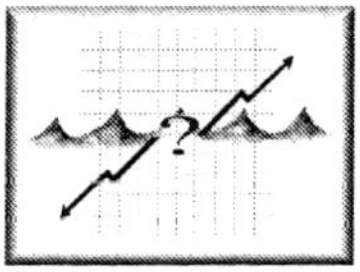

Jr., New York, NY: Simon & Schuster, c1998

Harry Dent's The H.S. Dent Forecast is a newsletter published monthly by the H.S. Dent Foundation, designed to give direction and guidance to both individual investors and financial professionals in the dramatically changing world of investing. Using exciting new research; developed from years of hands-on business experience, Harry Dent predicts a refreshingly positive and understandable view of the future. For more information visit the H.S. Dent web site @ http://www.hsdent.com

Economics

Rothchild, Michael, Bionomics: Economy As An Ecosystem, New York: Henry Holt & Company, 1990.

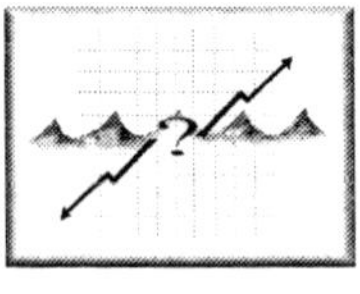

Samuelson, Paul Anthony, Nordhaus, William D., "Economics" New York: McGraw-Hill, c1985. Edition: 15th ed., 1995.

Kelly, Kevin, "New Rules For the New Economy: 10 Radical Changes for A Connected World," New York: Penguin Books, 1998.

Peter Bernstein's Economics & Portfolio Strategy newsletter provides authoritative and often controversial views on the economy and the capital markets, including the application of theoretical issues to hands-on portfolio management. It speaks the language of institutional investment professionals and sophisticated individual investors. For more information visit @ http://www.peterlbernsteininc.com/default.htm

.

Financial Advice Business

The financial advice business is built on the pillars of trust, integrity and ethics. Therefore, excellent advisor must develop ways to grow their business while maintaining these pillars of character. Here is the leading mind on financial practice development:

Murray, Nick, "The Excellent Investment Advisor," Sisco & Evans, Ltd., 1996. Additional information can be found @ http://www.nickmurray.com.

Focus Investing

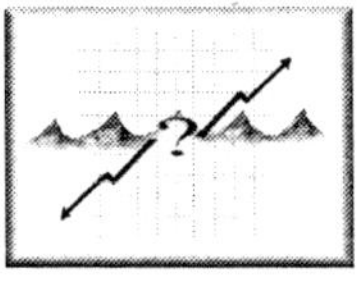

Focus investing is when an investor concentrates his investment picks in companies that he thinks have a high probability of outperforming stock market. Pursuing this strategy requires patience and intellectual fortitude because it is a strategy that is the different than how investors think today..

Hagstrom, Robert, "The Essential Buffet," New York: John Wiley & Sons, 2001.

Hagstrom, Robert, Latticework; "The New Investing," New York; John Wiley & Sons, 2001.

Investment Classics

Berkshire Hathaway, Annual Reports 1977 –2000 can be found @ http://www.berkshirehathaway.com/letters/letters.html

Fisher, Phillip, "Common Stocks and Uncommon Profits," New York: Harper & Brothers, 1958.

Graham, Benjamin, "The Intelligent

Investor: a Book of Practical Counsel," New York, Harper [1959], [2d rev. ed.]

Graham, Benjamin, "Security Analysis; Principles and Technique" [by] Benjamin Graham, David L. Dodd [and] Sidney Cottle. With the collaboration of Charles Tatham, New York, McGraw-Hill [1962], 4th ed

Lefevre, Edwin, "Reminiscences of a Stock Operator" by Edwin Lefèvre; with an introd. by Joseph M. Stabile [s.l.]: Citadel Financial Enterprises, [1976?], c1923

Schwed, Fred Jr., "Where are the Customers' Yachts?": A Good Hard Look at Wall Street, New York: Simon and Schuster, 1940.

Siegel, Jeremy J, "Stocks For the Long Run: The Definitive Guide to Financial Market

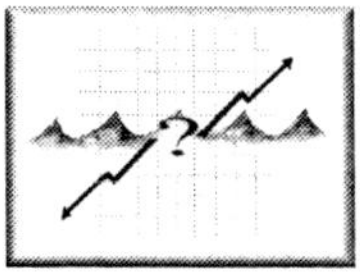

Returns and Long-term Investment Strategies," New York: McGraw-Hill, c1998, 2nd ed.

Investment Wisdom

(OTHER GREAT BOOKS WORTH READING)

Bernstein, Peter L., "Against the Gods: The Remarkable Story of Risk," New York: John Wiley & Sons, 1996.

Bernstein, Peter L., "Capital ideas: The Improbable Origins of Modern Wall Street," New York: Free Press; Toronto: Maxwell Macmillan Canada; New York: Maxwell Macmillan International, 1992

Dreman, David, "Contrarian Investment Strategies," New York, NY, Simon & Schuster, 1998.

Lynch, Peter (Peter S.), "Beating the

Street," Peter Lynch with John Rothchild, New York: Simon & Schuster, c1993

Lynch, Peter (Peter S.), "One Up on Wall Street: How to Use What You Already Know to Make Money In the Market," New York: Simon and Schuster, 1989.

MUTUAL FUNDS

Further insight on mutual fund investing can be found in Jack Bogle's book. Bogle is a senior chairman and founder of the Vanguard Group, one of the two largest mutual fund organizations in the world. Bogle presents a platform for intelligent investing and then uncovers the ills that beset the mutual fund industry, serious ills that thwart our efforts to accumulate adequate financial resources. Bogle analyzes costs, scrutinizes asset size, exposes tax inefficiencies, warns of "empty suit" directors, and reveals the severe conflict between fund principles and fund pro-motion.

Bogle, John C., "Common Sense on Mutual Funds: New Imperatives for the Intelligent Investor," 1999

Persistence of Performance

Studies show that there is no significant available evidence that will help investors locate next year's top performing mutual fund. Bouncing from one hot fund to another hot fund based on price performance does nothing to aid investors in growing money.

Mark Cahart, "On Persistence in Mutual Fund Performance," Journal of Finance, vol. 52, no. 1, March 1997.

Darryll Hendricks, Javendu Patel and Richard Zeckhauser, "Hot Hands in Mutual Funds: Short-Run Persistence of Relative Performance, 1974-1988," Journal of Finance, vol. 48, no. 1, March 1993.

Stephen Brown and William Goetzmann, "Performance Persistence," Journal of Finance, vol. 50, no. 2, June 1995.

POINT & FIGURE CHARTING

Dr. Carroll Aby, Jr., "Point & Figure Charting The Complete Guide," 1996, Traders Press, Inc.

Thomas Dorsey, "Point & Figure Charting The Essential Application for Forecasting and Tracking Market Prices 2nd

Edition," Marketplace Books, John Wiley & Sons, 2001.

Tom Dorsey also offers a web site called Point & Figure University @ http://208.149.108.6/cgi-bin/foxweb.exe/d:/foxapps/fwunivin which an investor can learn all about P&F techniques.

Return Assumption in Allegory

All returns and hypothetical assumption of portfolio values were consistent with data from the InvestmentView software package distributed for commercial use by Weisenberger a Division of Thompson Financial. *On page 72 and 76 of "Optimist Versus Pessimist," the indices used for 50-year historical returns (Dec. 31st 1951 to Dec 31st 2001) were the S&P 500 Composite*

Total Return Index for stocks, the Lehman Brothers Long-Term Government Index for bonds and the 3 month Treasury Bond Yield for cash (bills) and Consumer Price Index (CPI) for inflation.

Sell Discipline

For a description of sell discipline reference:

Donald L. Cassidy, "It's When You Sell That Counts," The McGraw Hill Companies, 1997.

Valuation

Most analysts who use multiples use them in conjunction with "comparable" firms, to form conclusions about whether firms are fairly valued or not. The analysis begins with two deci-

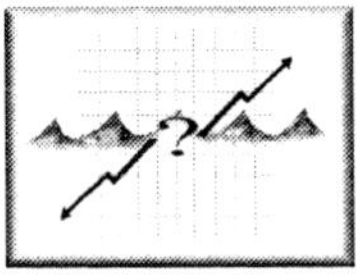

sions: (1) the multiple that will be used in the analysis (i.e. price-to-earnings, price-to-book, price-to-cash flow, etc. . .) and (2) the group of firms that will comprise the comparable firms. Discounted cash flow (DCF) or intrinsic valuation is the value of any assets as a function of the cash flow it generates, the life of the asset, the expected growth in the cash flows and the riskiness associated with the cash flows. For a excellent guide to valuation please refer to:

Aswath Damodaran, "Investment Valuation," John Wiley & Sons, New York, 1996. You can also visit Damodaran's web site @ http://www.stern.nyu.edu/~adamodar/

WALL STREET RESEARCH, ANALYSTS

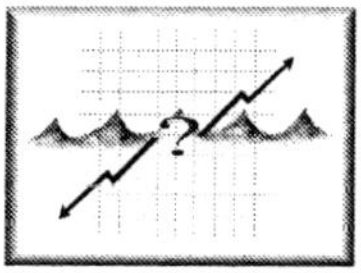

The allegory letter from analyst Fairly

Bleeker is an attempt to expose conflicts of interest that exist on Wall Street For "real-world" insight on conflicts on Wall Street reference the following:

"How Did So Many Get It So Wrong?" Gretchen Morgenson, New York Times, Dec. 31, 2001

"Bad Advice," Faith Keenan, Bloomberg, July 2000

"JP Morgan Reins in the Analysts," The Times, March 21, 2001

"Conflict of Interest and the Credibility of Underwrite Analyst Recommendations," Roni Michaely and Kent L. Womack, Feb. 1999

"The Numbers Game," David Henry, Business Week, May 14, 2001

"How Can Analysts Maintain Their

Independence?" Acting SEC Chairman Laura S. Unger, April 19, 2001

May 14th, 2001 issue of Fortune with cover titled, "Can We Ever Trust Wall Street Again." With articles: "Where Mary Meeker Went Wrong" by Peter Elkind; "Betrayal on Wall Street" by Shawn Tully; "Hear No Risk, See No Risk, Speak No Risk" by Bethany McLean; "Diary of a Financial Pornographer" by Nelson Schwartz.

Wealth

Definition of wealth in the allegory is adapted from thoughts of:

John-Roger & Peter McWilliams, "Wealth 101," 1992: Prelude Press.

ABOUT THE AUTHOR

Walt Sokira has been a financial professional since 1985. He has advised hundreds of investors with cumulative wealth well over half-billion dollars. He is owner, Portfolio Strategist and Senior Private Portfolio Manager of WALT ST Investment Management, Ltd. a specialized money management firm that provides private portfolio management to investment advisors and their clients. Walt resides in Northeast Ohio with his wife Jennifer who is also the President of WALT ST Investment Management, Ltd. with their four children: Abby, Kevin, Paige, Andrea. To reach the author you can write him at 5611 Hudson Drive, Suite #400 Hudson, Ohio 44236 or email him at walt@waltst.com.

NO BULL INVESTMENT POINTS

1) Wealth is more than money. It is health and happiness. It is loving, caring and sharing. It is prosperity and abundance. It is knowing what we want and enjoying what we have. Wealth is more than money — but money sure is nice.

2) Watch your step. To be successful and reach the pasture of financial serenity you must walk through the woods and the fields — and there are a lot of bear and bull stink piles.

3) A pessimist has trouble seeing the opportunities of the market — an optimist has trouble seeing the risks.

4) When the story breaks down move on.

5) Set an objective for your portfolio that is focused on growing money not percentages.

6) Don't fear . . . maximize your stock allocation.

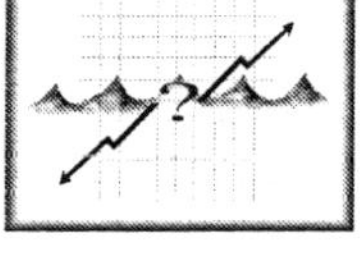

7) Select stocks that demonstrate the economic reality of your money objective. The best benchmark for a portfolio is a constantly monitored focused list of stocks with improving economics.

8) Use the art of diversification to build concentrated, focused portfolios of 15 to 25 individual stocks

9) Sectors are sexy and deserve strategic attention when building a focused portfolio.

10) Stock your pond. Constantly refining a universe of your best ideas will keep you from wasting valuable time on what to buy.

11) Paying for results is never painful and often it helps keep the pond stocked.

12) Comparative analysis can provide some of the meat that you are looking for when valuing stocks. Take the price divided by the economic weight (revenues, earnings, book value, dividends and cash flow) and compare, compare and compare.

13) Understand and utilize the power of discounted cash flow analysis (DCF). For the long-